G000152868

I BELIEVE IN TAKING ACTION

I Believe in

Taking Action

Steve Chalke

Hodder & Stoughton
LONDON SYDNEY AUCKLAND

Copyright © 1996 Steve Chalke.

First published in Great Britain 1996.

The right of Steve Chalke to be identified as the Author of the Work has been asserted by him in accordance with the Copyright, Designs and Patents Act 1988.

Scripture quotations taken from the HOLY BIBLE,
NEW INTERNATIONAL VERSION. Copyright © 1973, 1978, 1984 by International Bible Society. Used by permission of Hodder & Stoughton Ltd. All rights reserved. 'NIV' is a registered trademark of International Bible Society. UK trademark number 1448790. Those quotations not taken from the NIV are original translations.

10 9 8 7 6 5 4 3 2 1

All rights reserved. No part of this publication may be reproduced, stored in a retrieval system, or transmitted, in any form or by any means without the prior written permission of the publisher, nor be otherwise circulated in any form of binding or cover other than that in which it is published and without a similar condition being imposed on the subsequent purchaser.

British Library Cataloguing in Publication Data
A record for this book is available from the British Library.

ISBN 0 340 66144 5

Designed and typeset by Kenneth Burnley at Irby, Wirral, Cheshire.
Printed and bound in Great Britain by Cox & Wyman Ltd, Reading, Berkshire

Hodder and Stoughton Ltd
A division of Hodder Headline PLC
338 Euston Road, London NW1 3BH

Contents

Editor's preface

THIS NEW SERIES is intended to build on the widely acknowledged success of the original 'I Believe' series, of which several volumes continue to be in print. Now as then, each book sets out to tackle one of the key issues which faces Christians today. The overall aim is to stimulate informed thinking and to encourage living faith by building a bridge between the ever relevant teaching of the Bible and the complex realities of the modern world.

Steve Chalke is one of the most skilled bridge-builders in Britain today. Through his work in the media, not least as resident 'vicar' on ITV's national breakfast programme, he has reached millions with the vitality of his Christian faith. Such exposure in the media is far from being merely a carefully cultivated image. Steve's passion for the practical outworking of the gospel led him to found the Oasis Trust a decade or so ago, an organisation that has done much costly and pioneering work in helping Christians demonstrate the love of Christ to their needy neighbours in society.

Those looking for easy answers and instant solutions will not find them here. This book sets an example of how commitment to the pressing issues of the day needs to be rooted in painstaking research and prayerful reflection. Only then is it possible for us to take action which will help rather than hinder. It's good too to see the encouragement to act in partnership with others rather than trying to go it alone. I am most grateful to Steve for what he shares in this book, and expect it to help many, not only to think and talk about what is wrong with our society, but to take effective action as well.

David Stone

Introduction

Engaging our culture

**'Christian asceticism called the world evil
and abandoned it.
Humanity is waiting for a Christian revolution
which will call the world evil and change it.'**

American theologian Walter Rauschenbusch

THE TASK OF THE CHURCH in any culture is always to engage it without being engulfed by it. We are called to walk the difficult road of being what Jesus described in John 17 as 'in' but not 'of' the world. This is a responsibility which will always stretch us by continually demanding our best thinking and our most positive response to society around us, rather than our withdrawal from it.

To achieve this biblical pattern of involvement – engaging our culture without compromising our faith – we must take two vital preparatory steps, both of which require us to listen rather than make premature pronouncements:

1. We must learn to listen to the world around us, working hard to understand our culture.
2. We must reflect on that culture, its values and direction, in the light of the Bible and its teaching.

Only as we commit ourselves wholeheartedly to *both* of these disciplines – first listening, then reflecting – will we ever be equipped to respond to our culture with anything more than knee-jerk reactions. Only then will we be in a position to engage and communicate biblical principles effectively to the post-Christian, post-literate and post-modern culture in which we live.

Christians are good at talking. We've got something to say and we want to say it. In fact, it goes much deeper than that: we've been entrusted with a message, and it's our responsibility to share it. We can't keep silent. We are called to speak out, to spread the good news, to proclaim God's word, to fulfil the Great Commission, and to be who we are: witnesses. We understand Paul's desperate cry, 'I am compelled, anguished if I don't preach the gospel' (1 Cor. 9:16).

But imagine a person who wanders into a Paris bakery for the first time, totally unprepared for the fact that, quite reasonably, they're going to be faced with a sales assistant who speaks no English. They make their request slowly, in carefully pronounced English with just the hint of a French accent.

'Have you got any bread?'

No response. They try again, this time in firmer, slower, louder tones.

'Have . . . you . . . got . . . any . . . *bread*?'

The assistant still looks blank.

The whole exercise is repeated again, but this time with even more volume, hand actions, and a forced smile to cover the frustration.

'Bread. B - R - E - A - D. BREAD! Yes?'

The result? For all the energy used, the shopkeeper still looks as blank as ever.

As every parent knows from bitter experience, if someone honestly doesn't understand you when you ask them to do something, there's no point in making the same request again in the same way . . . only louder: it's totally counter-productive, and it only raises everyone's stress levels. No amount of shouting will succeed in getting you heard. Instead, you need to stop, listen, and rethink your method and style of communication. This, and only this, will enable you to change your verbal and body language, express things differently, and make yourself properly understood.

Too often, when we've preached what we regard as 'the Word' and not been understood by our audience, our response has simply been to shout louder. If the world is not hearing us, we reason, it's because of *their* 'spiritual deafness', not *our* inability to communicate. 'The powers of this world have blinded their eyes and blocked their ears,' we convince ourselves. But before automatically jumping to this somewhat premature conclusion, wouldn't it at least be sensible to check if we ourselves are the ones with the problem?

> **'Christians are a dim, ego-tripping minority which is dead set on telling everybody why they ought to become Christians, instead of finding out why they aren't.'**
>
> Australian journalist Max Harris

Remaining faithful to Scripture is only half of our task. And on its own, it's never enough. We need to communicate biblical truth in ways that ordinary people can understand. Advising his followers about how to address 'plain people' back in the eighteenth century, John Wesley insisted that 'we should constantly use the most common, little, easy words which our language affords'. If, when we tell them about Jesus, the 'plain people' of today look at us with the same bewilderment the Paris shopkeeper showed the English-speaking customer, the reason is often simple: we're not speaking their language. Just as it makes sense to learn some basic French if we want to communicate effectively in a Paris bakery, so we will have to invest time and energy in learning the language and understanding the world-view of those outside the Church if we want to communicate effectively with them.

We read in John 1:14 that 'the Word became human and made his home among us'. Everything God wanted to say to us was wrapped up in Jesus, who delivered his message by becoming a human being. As Paul says, Jesus was willing to make himself nothing by 'taking the nature of a servant' (Phil. 2:6–7). Rather than insisting on remaining as *he* was, God became as *we are* in order to rescue us. Jesus was born into a specific culture, at a specific time in history, speaking a specific language and living within a specific community of people. He didn't patronisingly expect his audience to accommodate themselves to his language and customs; instead he accommodated himself to theirs. Only after thirty years spent understanding and living in his culture was he ready to begin speaking to it, clothing eternal truth in stories, phrases and terminology that made sense to his audience. Indeed, this is what incarnation is: not simply, as it's often weakly and inadequately expressed, that God became a human being, but rather that he became a very specific human being.

The clear implication of all this is that God's word is *only* God's word when it's both theologically sound and culturally relevant. One of its hallmarks is that it makes sense and communicates to its target audience. So if the Church offers society anything less, it falls short of being both biblical and Christian: and evangelical, for that matter!

This is a tough issue to grapple with. Theologically, it's the tension between 'transcendence' and 'immanence'; between an eternal message and an ever-changing world. The gospel of Jesus is absolute truth. And absolute truth is eternal. Like God, it's the same yesterday, today and for ever. But, as John reminds us, in Jesus absolute truth 'became a human being', stepping into a specific time and culture. In order to be relevant, in other words, the word had to become real in the 'here and now'. Jesus was the eternal Word of God, but he was also a first-century Palestinian Jew, from a poor carpenter's family in an insignificant northern town in a despised outback colony of the mighty Roman Empire.

Truth is eternal, but its expressions are relative, and must be constantly changing to keep up with an ever-evolving culture. If it's to be authentically Christian, truth must be incarnated. So if we are to speak truth to our present generation – our culture – we will have to learn what that culture is like by listening to it carefully.

As one TV producer put it to me: 'The problem with you Christians is, you're always trying to answer Question No. 17 when the rest of us aren't even sure what Question No. 1 is. You need to begin where we are, not where you want us to be. Some of you are even worse than the politicians. It makes no difference what the question is, because you never answer it. You always tell us what you want us to hear anyway.'

Of course, we should never make the mistake of thinking that our task is somehow to adapt the gospel to make it relevant. The gospel is *always* relevant, because it's eternal truth. Instead, our task is to let it live and breathe as incarnated truth, not allowing its relevance to be hindered by imprisoning it in outdated, archaic and irrelevant language, traditions and mindsets. We must constantly work hard to liberate it from historical trappings for a new generation. And to do this, we must listen to our culture rather than abandoning it.

But our task is not just to *listen* to our culture. It's also to analyse it, to *reflect* on it biblically. As John Stott claims in his book *The Contemporary Christian*, we need to 'double-listen', a skill which he defines as 'the faculty of listening to two voices at the same time, the voice of God through Scripture and the voices of men and women around us'. This, he adds, is 'indispensable to Christian discipleship and Christian mission'. In the oft-quoted words of Charles Spurgeon, 'the Christian preacher is one who carries the Bible in one hand, the newspaper in the other . . . and reads both'. But today, much of our preaching – often, tragically, even preaching that proudly labels itself 'exegetical' – is marked by a sad lack of application and understanding of our culture.

'If God had intended us to pickle our brains and put them aside, if he hadn't wanted us to struggle with the great issues of human history and culture, then he would not have sent us a middle-eastern book spanning many centuries and cultures – he would have sent us a small tract.'

Australian biker minister John Smith

Aldous Huxley once wrote that most of a person's life was 'one prolonged effort to prevent oneself thinking'. As Christians, we have more temptation than most *not* to think. The philosopher Bertrand Russell mocked that 'most Christians would rather die than think – in fact, they do!' American sociology professor and ordained Baptist minister, Tony Campolo, remembers growing up in an atmosphere where doctrine was spoon-fed and independent thinking discouraged: 'Sound? I was so sound I believed in the Virgin Birth even before I knew what a virgin was!'

In his recent book, *Fit Bodies, Fat Minds*, leading evangelical thinker Os Guinness argues that evangelical Christians have actually been *encouraged* away from real thinking about their faith and society by the theology they've inherited from their predecessors. 'Ever since the eighteenth century,' he says, 'we evangelicals have had a natural bias towards empty brains and happy hearts.'

The lives of men like Isaiah and the other Old Testament prophets stand in marked contrast to this. Known as the great 'statesman prophet', Isaiah was a man with an in-depth grasp of God's word given through Moses, matched and balanced by a clear understanding of the contemporary socio-political situation in Judah, neighbouring Israel, and all the surrounding nation states. This ability to 'double-listen' was what equipped him for his God-given prophetic task. Only the same breadth of understanding will be sufficient to equip today's Church for a similar task: to be God's irrepressible voice to our nation and its leaders. Tragically, however, the gift of prophecy has been silenced by non-use in one wing of the Church, and so minimised by abuse in the other that, in many cases, it now amounts to little more than a kind of spiritual back-slapping.

'The prophet is a person on the street, the person who judges history from the viewpoint of God.'

Salvadoran theologian Jon Sobrino

There is much to learn from the way in which Jesus reprimanded the Sadducees and Pharisees, whom he called 'blind guides'. Although they set themselves up as spiritual leaders, they lacked the discernment which comes from 'double-listening'. 'When evening comes,' he told them, 'you say, "It will be fair weather, for the sky is red," and in the morning, "Today it will be stormy, for the sky is red and overcast." You know how to interpret the appearance of the sky, but you cannot interpret the signs of the times' (Matt. 16: 1–4; cf. Luke 12:54–57).

Finally, having listened to our culture, and reflected on it in the light of God's word, we will be ready to engage it in the certainty that, in doing so, we will fulfil our distinctive prophetic role to be light in the darkness.

At Pentecost, when the Holy Spirit came over the disciples, they began to 'speak in tongues'. But taking into account the huge amount of controversy this would later produce, why on earth didn't God choose to give them a 'safer' manifestation of the Spirit's presence? Wasn't there some way to produce the spectacular evangelistic result he wanted without all the subsequent hassle?

The truth is that 'tongues' were the obvious – in fact the *only* appropriate – gift for the occasion. Why? Because these 'tongues' weren't the kind that charismatics and anti-charismatics have spent so long tragically fighting over – they were something completely different. Far from being the 'tongues of angels' needing interpretation to make them intelligible, these were ordinary languages, instantly comprehensible to those around. As the crowd that had gathered from across the Middle East pointed out, 'all these people speaking are Galileans, aren't they? So how come each of us hears in our own mother tongue?'

> ### 'In the book of Acts, the coming of the Spirit kindled not only spiritual renewal but social revolution.'
>
> Sojourners leader Jim Wallis

The Holy Spirit was given to equip the Church for its mission: the task of presenting the good news about Jesus to every man, woman and child in a way they can understand and relate to; i.e., in their own language and culture. What happened on the Day of Pentecost, when the Spirit was poured out, was a symbol of the task facing the Church in the coming centuries.

The God-given responsibility to 'go' to all peoples, culturally as well as physically and speaking their language, is demonstrated again, in a different way, in Acts 17. When he arrived in a new town, Paul always made a habit of going to the synagogue first, to explain the good news to the Jews and 'God-fearing Gentiles' – his people. Only then did he go to the ordinary Gentiles in the marketplace. By comparing his speech to the synagogue at Pisidian Antioch (Acts 13) with that to the Gentiles in Athens (Acts 17), we get some idea of the extent to which Paul adapted his expression of the gospel to his audience. In Pisidian Antioch, he used Hebrew thought-patterns and quotations from the Old Testament to show that Jesus is the fulfilment of God's promises. But in Athens, he addressed the people using their own poetry, religious symbols and culture.

But though our task is to listen to our culture, it would be a mistake to assume that this should be done in the same way as we listen to God's word. To quote John Stott again, 'we listen to the word with humble reverence, anxious to understand it, and resolved to believe and obey what we understand. We listen to the world with critical alertness, anxious to understand it too, and resolved not necessarily to believe and obey it, but to sympathise with it and seek grace to discover how the gospel relates to it.'

Our task is to understand the world, to listen to it and learn its language, but never to capitulate to its trends and demands. 'Don't become moulded by this world,' said Paul (Rom. 12:2). The Church speaks most authentically to the world, not when it's indistinguishable from it, but when its distinctive light shines brightest. The Christian message is one of change. Listening to our culture with an open mind doesn't mean always having to agree with it.

This whole area has been a big problem for the Church. We have watched as some Christians, anxious to listen and respond to the world's agenda, have slowly surrendered to its standards and principles. We have seen the gospel not only compromised, but altogether lost as the distinctiveness of the Christian approach has vanished almost without trace.

The big question is, therefore: How can we be orthodox in our theology and yet radical in our application of it? The answer can only be: to *listen* hard to our culture, and then *reflect* on it with equal commitment, analysing it through the lens of Scripture and allowing the Holy Spirit to revolutionise our understanding. As evangelical bishop J. C. Ryle put it, when he attacked the fear of worldliness that underlay evangelicalism in the Victorian era:

When St Paul says, 'Come out and be separate,' he did not mean that Christians ought to take no interest in anything on earth except religion. To neglect science, art, literature and politics – to read nothing which is not directly spiritual – to know nothing about what is going on among mankind, and never to look at a newspaper – to care nothing about the government of one's own country, and to be utterly indifferent to the persons who guide its counsels and make its laws – all this may seem very right and proper in the eyes of some people. But I take leave to think that it is an idle, selfish neglect of duty.

The reality is that the greater the depth with which we understand the principles behind the flow of God's dealings with the human race – and especially the incarnation – the clearer it becomes that those most committed to an orthodox theology are compelled by that very fact to be radical in their application of Scripture and social involvement.

This book looks at several major contemporary issues, examining how we should respond biblically and effectively to each at both the national and local levels. In each chapter we will:

• Listen to the issues with a mixture of comment and current thinking from the world of politics, education, industry, medicine, media etc.
• Reflect carefully on each issue raised, drawing out important biblical principles and guidelines for our thinking and our response as Christians.
• Engage, applying these principles and looking at practical models and suggestions for an appropriate response.

At the end of each chapter, there is help on where to go for further advice and information.

Chapter 1

Unemployment

IF ALL WORK AND NO PLAY makes Jack a dull boy, what does all play and no work make of him? Unemployment is a very complex problem, but not one which is particularly high on most of our church agendas. Often the church's response is limited to something like a drop-in centre a couple of days a week; we might even have established a counselling service to help the unemployed talk through their problems, or give them gifts during harvest festival, and pray for them every Sunday. We give the unemployed pastoral help, but what they *really* want are jobs. This, you might think, is not our concern: think again.

Listen

Paid work, and therefore the lack of available paid work (unemployment), have been around for thousands of years. They were even evident in the parable of the workers in the vineyard (Matt. 20), but have only been dominant in Europe for a few centuries. At the time of the Reformation, for instance, the feudal system was still in full swing. The majority of jobs were in the countryside, and most people worked for a share of the crop on their master's land.

Trading, a profession as old as the hills, steadily increased with time, especially after the exploration of America, Africa and the East by Spain and Portugal. But it was only with the industrial revolution that paid employment as we understand it became widespread. Industry has slowly produced a rise in general living standards; but it has brought in its wake, for the first time, the spectre of mass unemployment.

In our own time we are seeing a microchip revolution whose impact on the current workplace is as great as that of the industrial revolution on the eighteenth century! This time, however, the upheaval is caused not by mechanisation but by technology.

> **'If there is a technological advance without social advance, there is, almost automatically, an increase in human misery.'**
>
> Economist Michael Harrington

Most economic analysts and sociologists are agreed that the unemployment problem we now face is very complex: industrial specialisation, automation, recession, the fight against inflation, the decline of traditional manufacturing industries, and increasing foreign competition all combine to create a dragon we seem virtually powerless to slay.

A survey in *The Economist* for instance (October 1994), using World Bank figures, estimates that in the next twenty-five years, the share of world output of the rich industrial nations will fall from 55 per cent to 38 per cent, as the share of developing countries (including the former Eastern Bloc) rises from 45 per cent to 62 per cent. China will replace the USA as having the 'largest economy' in the world, and Britain will fall from eighth to fourteenth in the same scales. Seven of the ten largest economies in the world will be in Asia.

Most jobs created in the last decade have been part-time, and most of these are filled by women. Part-time work can suit a lot of people, such as those who have taken early retirement, those with minor medical problems, or those with children or relatives to look after. But some people are forced by economic need to take part-time jobs when they are really after something permanent.

The self-employed can often find it hard to get enough work to pay their bills and overhead expenses, especially during a recession. And although the hardest hit have been the unskilled, the semi-literate and manual workers, unemployment amongst university graduates has risen in recent years. Many students find themselves having to take jobs for which they are over-qualified, shunting aside those better suited to this employment. As the student joke goes: What do you say to a graduate with a job? Big Mac and large fries, please.

In addition to this, rising numbers of those in middle management find themselves made redundant during cutbacks, and then unable to find appropriate work. And at the bottom of the pile in terms of qualifications and experience, school leavers are finding it more and more difficult to find either work or a place on a training scheme, in spite of the government's pledge to ensure this.

Though unemployment touches many sectors of society, the most serious worry must be the long-term unemployed, those who have been out of work for more than one year. These are doubly hit, not only by the financial deprivations, boredom and lack of self-esteem which inevitably accompany unemployment, but also by their lack of appeal to employers. The longer a person has been unemployed, the harder it becomes for them to find work. The long-term unemployed tend to be less skilled, less qualified, less educated, and less confident; all things likely to put off a prospective employer. Long-term unemployment brings in its wake extra poverty. A recent leader in *The Guardian* reported that the suicide rate among the unemployed is eleven times higher than among the rest of society.

Under the leadership of Tony Blair, the British Labour Party has restated its aim to create 'full employment'. What this means in practice is an unemployment rate of 3 per cent of the workforce, but with no long-term unemployment. It's questionable, of course, whether or not this is possible. The 'era of full employment' between 1945 and about 1975 may yet turn out to have been a passing phase, dead and gone like the dinosaurs: we may find ourselves, like King Canute, trying to turn back an inevitable tide. If this is the case, we will have to rethink our approach to work quite radically, moving away from seeing pay as all-important.

If we are to behave morally, we must support the hardest hit. All the major political parties are considering welfare reforms, in an attempt to cut down on public spending and target benefit where it is needed most. They are concerned that welfare might otherwise prove to be a bottomless pit, and that the system should not be seen to support those with no intention of working – a perennial fear which a growing amount of recent research has shown to be unfounded. Most unemployed people want work, not welfare.

According to a study done by the Methodist Church Division of Social Responsibility:

- In 1950, shortly after the creation of the welfare state, the population was around fifty million, thirty million of working age; of that, sixteen million were employed and only 300,000 were unemployed.
- In 1993 the population was closer to sixty million, thirty-seven million of working age; of that, twenty-four million were employed and three million were registered as unemployed.
- A further three million were 'economically inactive'; that is, disabled people, single mothers and the like, who received benefit but were not available for work.

According to a government published study of July 1994:

- Almost a quarter of the total population is receiving income-related benefit.
- Twelve per cent (4.55 million) of those in work live below the poverty line (less than 50 per cent of the national average income after housing costs); this is triple the 1979 figure.
- Three-quarters of unemployed people live below this poverty line.

According to the Labour Force Survey for the winter 1993–94:

- 122,500 16–17 year olds are unemployed; this is 10 per cent of the 16–17-year-old population, and 17.4 per cent of those aged 16–17 able to work.
- Of this, 90,400 (74 per cent) have no income, in spite of the government's pledge that every teenager should be in work or in training.
- London (17.4 per cent), Northern Ireland (18.9 per cent) and the North (14.6 per cent) are hit the most by unemployment.
- Twice as many men as women are unemployed who have looked for work within four weeks of being surveyed.

Reflect

The Bible has little to say about unemployment, but a great deal to say about work.

Although many people consider that they work only in order to earn a living, as though work were a drudgery introduced with the Fall, the book of Genesis presents a very different perspective. In chapter 2, we are told that God finishes the *work* of creation, and that humans are placed in the garden to *work* it. We are specifically told that God *works*. Far from being a curse, for the writers of Genesis work is something *creative*.

God's creation is not something completed, but something ongoing in which we play a part. When God created the world, he had in mind a place in which everything lives harmoniously together. But, not wishing to be surrounded by robots, he decided to involve human beings in the creative process by giving them free will and work to do. We are co-*workers* with God in creation. Work is therefore always meant to be creative: something which adds to the world, and an integral part of God's overall act of creation.

> **'To work, to transform this world, is to become somebody and to build the human community.'**
>
> Peruvian theologian Gustavo Gutierrez

Work is not only part of creation, however; it also gives us *identity*. When we meet somebody new, one of the first things we ask them is, 'What do you do?' Work is a considerable factor in determining who we are as a person, and how we are seen by the rest of society. When Jesus taught in his home town, for instance, the people there asked, 'But isn't this the *carpenter's* son?' (Matt. 13:55). They couldn't see past Jesus' occupation (which at the time would inevitably have been that of his father), because a person's occupation defined who they were and how they fitted in.

This is why unemployment is so much more than the loss of a secure income. Unemployed people feel not only that society doesn't value them (because they are unable to do something which contributes to society, and is paid in return); they often feel unsure any longer of who they are.

In order for work to contribute positively to someone's identity, it must bring them an element of *dignity*. Proverbs 31 says that the work of a good woman should bring her universal praise. Paul told the Christians of Thessalonica that manual work would bring them 'the respect of outsiders' (1 Thess. 4:11).

I worked in a factory for over a year where the most demanding thing I had to do each day was to clock on and clock off. The job gave me no satisfaction, and no dignity. I had no real opportunity to contribute the skills and talents I had. Too often, especially with 'unskilled' work, people are treated as though they were robots. The sad thing is, many people have come to accept this as inevitable.

'If God has given all people skills and brains to use, we cannot be happy if people at work are simply asked to be less efficient robots.'

Bishop David Sheppard

Tony Campolo tells the story of his father, who was a radio cabinet maker. When he started working, Tony's father crafted each radio casing carefully by hand. He loved his job. The work gave him the chance to create, and to be involved in what he did. He was a craftsman, and it gave him pride. Then came automation. And instead of making cabinets himself, Mr Campolo Sr supervised the *machine* which made them. 'My father no longer worked with tools, which are instruments used by people,' Tony recalls; 'instead he ran machines, which are instruments that use people.'

In fact, Karl Marx put it in much the same way: 'The labourer does not employ the means of production,' he wrote in *Das Capital*, 'but the means of production employ the labourer.' He called this process 'alienation'. And although we are used to seeing Marx as an enemy of the Church, we would do well to listen to these words. For in spite of his avowed atheism, much of Marx's thinking ironically has its roots in the Bible. For instance, Genesis warns of the alienation introduced by the Fall, which, whilst it didn't introduce work, certainly changed it for the worse. Work shouldn't be a burden which alienates people from themselves, from each other, from nature and from God, but something good which contributes to God's ongoing creation.

The absence of work is also destructive, because work forms part of our contribution to the overall work of God. That's why it shouldn't be allowed to become the privilege of a few, but *a basic right* granted to all people.

Before the Reformation, if somebody had a 'vocation', a 'calling', it meant that God intended them to become a priest or a nun. Even now, if we speak of someone 'receiving the call', we are usually referring not to the telephone but to the ordained ministry. But this wasn't always the case. When he started his order in 1210, St Francis of Assisi was keen that its members should *not* be priests. When the Pope insisted, Francis started a second order to provide a sense of vocation for ordinary people. Three hundred years later, the Protestant Reformers encouraged their flock to believe that whatever work they did – 'secular' or 'sacred' – was their vocation. In other words, even if we are not in what we too narrowly define as 'full-time Christian work', or ordained as a minister, our work is still part of God's work. It's still a vocation.

The Puritans took this idea to an art form. 'If you're called to be a trader,' they argued, 'you should be the best trader you possibly can be.' And the same went for any profession: butcher, banker, blacksmith, farmer, fieldhand, etc. Essentially, for the Puritans, work was a form of worship. You 'gave glory' to God by being excellent in your line of work. On the face of it, this sounds – and is – highly commendable. But over time, the definition of what it meant to be the 'best possible' trader, for instance, became confused and corrupted. Did a trader essentially make money or provide a service? All too often, the temptation to define a trader simply as a money-maker, and work as primarily a means of making money, was too great to resist.

R. H. Tawney argued that for some Puritans (though by no means all), 'a creed which transformed the acquisition of wealth from a drudgery or a temptation into a moral duty was the milk of lions,' since it meant that 'the good Christian was not wholly dissimilar from the economic man.' This issue remains a vital one today.

'They say hard work never hurt anybody, but I figure, why take the chance?'

Attributed to Ronald Reagan

The New Testament writers had an equivalent of this so-called 'Protestant work ethic'. The word 'liturgy', which we think of in terms of church worship, literally means 'the people's work'. Any kind of work which furthered the kingdom of God could be considered liturgy: from the priestly service of Zechariah (Luke 1:23) to the 'works of service' of the entire Corinthian church (2 Cor. 9:12). It was only when the Roman Empire adopted Christianity that autocracy crept into the Church, creating a split between the clergy and the people: *them* and *us*. In the early Church the people acted as one, everybody doing God's work. In fact, when a distinction *was* made (Acts 6), seven people were anointed, not to 'give attention to prayer and the ministry of the word', but to 'wait on tables'!

So a Christian doctrine of work is one of liturgy, of *everyone* working for the kingdom of God. But because unemployment effectively excludes people from the liturgy, it therefore denies them their vocation. Little wonder Archbishop William Temple called it 'the greatest social evil'.

Old Testament law (Leviticus 25) features something called the 'Jubilee'. If for some reason a person couldn't support themselves, they were entitled to sell their land – or even themselves – to someone else; every fiftieth year, all these debts were cancelled: both land and liberty were restored. This system ensured that no great injustice could last very long, although there is some doubt as to whether or not it was ever put into practice. In the meantime, however, at any time before the fifty years were up, any close male relative was entitled to 'redeem' them by paying their debt.

We see this 'redeemer' at work in Ruth 4, where Boaz took it on himself to redeem Ruth, even though he wasn't her closest male relative. In Job 19, God is shown to be the ultimate Redeemer. And the prophets tirelessly assured consecutive kings of Israel that they were to act as 'redeemers' for those who had no rich or powerful relatives. This is actually the main standard by which Old Testament kings were judged.

By siding with the poor against the religious leaders of his time, Jesus took on himself the same function. In fact, the title of 'Redeemer' that we give to Jesus draws its roots from this Old Testament custom. As Christians, therefore – people who have been entrusted with the task of carrying on Jesus' work – we too are called to be 'redeemers'.

The Church is faced with an enormous opportunity, and a huge responsibility, to place itself on the cutting edge once again in this task. In the nineteenth century, many Christians – especially evangelicals – responded to the challenge posed by such things as slavery, education, health care and child labour. Unemployment poses a similar challenge to today's Church, and we are clearly called to respond. The question is: How?

WORK

- Work is taking an active part in God's ongoing creation; it's what he made us for, and is therefore a source of identity and dignity.
- Work is a way of using the talents God has given us for the benefit of others, and is therefore a way of becoming part of the community.

UNEMPLOYMENT

- Unemployment, the absence of this work, is the denial of a God-given right and the squandering of God-given talent.
- Unemployment tells people that they are worthless, whilst God regards them as valued and loved.

Engage

Unemployment is such a deep and complex problem that we might be tempted to throw up our hands in despair, crying, 'What can I do?' The problem can seem overwhelming, but it's important to do *something*. But whatever you do, make sure that you keep within the following four guidelines.

1. *Work with other churches.* The first thing to understand is that, 'What can I do?' is the wrong question. The right question is: 'What can *we* do?' And this does not just mean our church, but the church in our area. In 1 Corinthians 12, Paul reminds us that the Spirit gives many different gifts for the good of the whole body of Christ. Whilst there will certainly be people in our church with skills and resources useful for helping the unemployed, we may not have *all* the skills and resources needed. It is important, therefore, to work with other local churches.

> **'Unemployment seems to take away the opportunity to make a useful contribution.'**
>
> Bishop David Sheppard

2. *Work with other organisations.* It's tempting for us to rush in, thinking that with Jesus on our side, we must have all the answers. However, life is not a John Wayne film, and we are not the cavalry. If we don't come to unemployed people aiming to serve them, we will simply be adding to their problems. If we're serious about serving unemployed people then we must be prepared to work with any organisation, Christian or not, that can help – such as the local statutory authorities. If we are to engage our culture, we can't then remove ourselves from it by creating our own, jealously guarded schemes. Nevertheless, there is a lot that we can do as a church.

3. *Be professional.* It's not enough, if unemployed people want an advice centre, to expect the minister to cope with this under the

heading of 'pastoral care'. It may be necessary to liaise with the local social services, perhaps embarking on a joint venture. When I was assistant minister of Tonbridge Baptist Church, we approached Kent Social Services about the joint funding of a qualified social worker, Barry, who was also a member of the church. Barry worked on the 'patch', under the auspices of both the church and the council. It's not enough, if English or literacy classes are called for, to expect members of the church to provide this without expert training, such as a TEFL (Teaching English as a Foreign Language) course. Christians and church groups are already seen as well-meaning amateurs by many local authorities and people in the caring professions. The last thing we should do is reinforce this impression.

4. *Don't approach with a hidden agenda.* Whilst we should by no means deny the gospel, and shouldn't seek to compromise our Christian principles, we must realise that helping unemployed people is not a mere *consequence* of preaching the gospel. In this context it *is* preaching and living the gospel. We shouldn't approach unemployed people pretending to serve if our motives are primarily to convert them.

What exists is possible

Ron Sider reminds us that 'what exists is possible'. If you have got this far and are wondering, 'But what can we *do*?', then read on. Here are some examples not just of what *can be* done, but of what *is being* done:

Peckham Evangelical Churches Action Network (PECAN) is an ecumenical project in South London which specialises in education and training. Seven recruiters knock on every door in the estate three times a year, inviting the unemployed to enrol on an Employment Preparation Course, helping them to improve their CVs, interview techniques and confidence. Since Peckham is ethnically diverse, with many people who cannot yet speak English, the project also runs courses in English for Speakers of Other Languages.

In addition, PECAN runs a jobclub, encouraging people to discover and hone their skills, and one-to-one adult literacy classes. The group funds its £250,000 turnover through individual and corporate sponsorship, including well-known companies, and is interested in helping similar projects to get off the ground in other parts of the country. They estimate that about one-third of their 'graduates' are now working.

Christians Unemployment Group (CHUG) is a much smaller outfit in South Yorkshire. They aim to encourage unemployed people to learn new skills and develop old ones. They train people to make furnishings and hand crafts to sell, organising small co-operative workshops to facilitate this.

Newham Community Renewal Programme provides much more than simply help to the unemployed. It offers hostel accommodation for young homeless people (who find it very hard to get another job); resettlement for offenders; 'handyman' services for elderly and disabled people; English classes; office and computer skill training; enterprise training for those starting a small business; conference, fax and computer services; and information exchange services for churches and other groups. They see employment as a means of regenerating the community.

Church Action With The Unemployed (CAWTU) is a national ecumenical charity established to help co-ordinate churches' response to unemployment. It is especially concerned with structural (long-term) unemployment, aiming to inform churches about unemployed people; to help them create practical projects in response; to link such projects together such that each can learn from the others; and to liaise with government departments and other official bodies, presenting to them the concerns Christians have about unemployment.

The *Bromley by Bow Centre* is housed in a rejuvenated URC church building. Some 600 people, including unemployed people, use the centre every week for its restaurant, nursery, gardens, dance classes, language classes or art workshop. They aim to turn a nearby derelict site into an adventure playground and urban nature reserve, and to build a health centre in the old tyre depot. There was no Grand Design: everything grew in response to the needs of the community. Sunday worship takes place under a tent-like 'worship canopy', emphasising that Jesus Christ is the beating heart of the centre.

In Philadelphia, USA, Tony Campolo has set up several employment initiatives, including a company which strips down defunct telephones and sells the active components back to the phone company; a print works; and a removals business. Funded and administered by Tony's *Evangelical Association for the Promotion of Education*, the companies are owned by the workers, who would otherwise be facing unemployment.

Oasis itself plans to launch an employment initiative. A silk screen printing company will employ several unemployed people from South London, of any faith or none, to produce premium quality, eco-friendly, designer greeting cards. The aim is to start small and, by ploughing the profits back into the company, expand the workforce and extend the range.

Further information

Agencies

CHUG publish a 'Starter Kit'. Revd Raymond Draper, The Rectory, Church Lane, Wickersley, Rotherham, South Yorkshire, S66 0ES. Tel: 01709 543111.

CAWTU publish numerous booklets designed to help churches see how they might become involved.

PECAN publish an excellent *Project Hatching Workbook* for advice on setting up social action projects. 2 Cottage Green, London, SE5 7ST. Tel: 0171-701 9844.

Books

Michael Moynaugh, *Making Unemployment Work* (Lion).

Fran Beckett, *Called to Action* (Fount paperbacks, HarperCollins, 1989).

John Stott, *Issues Facing Christians Today* (Marshalls, 1989).

Chapter 2

Teenage sexuality

The reason 8,000 girls under 16 become pregnant each year is that we've listened to so-called experts and tossed the moral standards in the bin.

Children are taught the mechanics of sex, not the emotions. They learn of lust, not love. Instead of encouraging young people to jump into bed, we should be teaching them the first fact of life: the best contraceptive is the word 'No!'

NOT, AS YOU MIGHT EXPECT, the words of a church leader: instead, an editorial in *The Sun* newspaper.

But how do we teach them to say 'No'? It's no good locking up our daughters in chastity belts and throwing away the keys – they will only learn how to pick the locks, or else use a junior hacksaw! Instead, our goal must be to *educate* young people about sex, to inform them of their choices and the possible consequences of these choices, and then to trust them to make their own decisions – even if we think these are the wrong decisions.

Listen

According to Freud, the Victorian era – the time of 'traditional family values' – was one of great double standards. People appeared to have a healthy sexuality, but underneath the surface they were tortured with repressed sexual desire. The history books seem to provide ample evidence that in this, at least, Freud was right. But what would he have made of our own time, when sex is out in the open and used to sell everything from magazines to ice cream? We are all exposed to a considerable amount of sexual stimuli every day, both blatant and concealed. Teenagers, who are trying to make sense of the world their parents have made, and their place in it, are especially vulnerable.

'O Lord, make me chaste . . . but not just yet.'

St Augustine

When young people hit puberty, any time between the ages of about 11 and 16, their hormones explode. Filled with emotions and impulses they've not experienced before, and usually convinced that they're the only people ever to have felt them quite so intensely, they are suddenly under enormous pressure:

- Young people are pressed by their own desires and emotions. Having emerged from an age at which the opposite sex seem less appealing than the thought of nuclear holocaust, they find themselves trying to come to terms with impulses and urges that are as bewildering as they are exciting.
- Young people are pressed to conform with their peers, amongst whom sex is a badge of honour. Sexual intercourse assumes almost mythical proportions. And although it's rarely as good as it promises to be, losing one's virginity is considered an essential part of being young. The pressure to do what you think all your friends are doing is intense, even when it turns out later that most of them aren't actually doing it. A recent survey by *Mizz* magazine revealed that whilst 45 per cent of readers had had sex before the age of 16, almost 85 per cent of readers thought that their *peers* had all had sex before this age. As *Mizz* concluded, 'It's official – other people have sex later than you think!'
- Young people are pressed by society, which teaches them that they should behave like adults: teenagers should be responsible and mature. More mature, perhaps, than their years. But to young people, the most important part of being an adult seems to be . . . sex. The adult world appears obsessed with sex, and our expectations that teenagers should behave like adults can push them toward having sex before they feel ready. It appears to be the short-cut to instant adulthood.

- Young people are pressed by the media, which uses sex to sell virtually anything. The human sexual instinct is exploited to make magazines, books, newspapers, television programmes, films, food, coffee, clothing, alcohol, music, skincare products, cars, holidays and a whole host of other things seem irresistibly attractive. In fact, almost the only thing sex is *not* used to advertise is baby products!

- Ironically, young people can be pressured into having sex by the way in which their parents set about telling them *not* to have sex. Struggling to come to terms with their independence, and to control their desires and emotions, young people can feel isolated and confused. Many become convinced that their parents don't understand what they're going through. In fact, in spite of obvious evidence to the contrary, most young people can't imagine their parents ever having had sex! Sometimes the way in which parents tell their children not to have sex can seem more like laying down the law than giving concerned advice.

> **'Kangaroos do it, dingos do it, flies do it; so you're not proving anything by doing it.'**
>
> Australian biker minister John Smith

This is why education is vital. Once relegated to the biology class and confined to the pure mechanics, sex education has recently been 'upgraded': emotional and social aspects *must* now be taught in schools, and, because of this, parents are allowed to remove their children from these lessons.

Although recent studies suggest that the number of teenage pregnancies is down from recent years, it's still much too high. According to the Family Planning Association (FPA), most of the 8,000 girls under 16 who get pregnant every year do so inadvertently, and wish that they hadn't. Many find out the hard way that the old wives' tales about not being able to get pregnant the first time you have sex, or if you stand up immediately afterwards, etc., aren't true. Others are the victims of ignorance and a lack of forward planning. In fact, according to the FPA, as many as 90 per cent of pregnant teenagers didn't even plan to have sex, much less a baby! It's the same with AIDS: although the government advertising campaign of the mid-1980s was relatively effective in teaching people the dangers of AIDS, most young people today are not old enough to remember it. They think that AIDS is an older person's disease, and that it could never happen to them. So they take no precautions when they have sex. For this reason, young people are most at risk from HIV and AIDS, as well as from a whole host of other sexually transmitted diseases (STDs). Their ignorance is both dangerous and depressing.

According to the Family Planning Association:

- Roughly 20 per cent of under-16s have had sex; this rises to 52 per cent of 16 year olds, 67 per cent of 17 year olds, and 83 per cent of 18–19 year olds.
- 6.9 per cent of all 15–19 year olds get pregnant.
- 55 per cent of those having first-time sex use no protection. 54 per cent of 16–24 year olds think that they're not at risk from AIDS.
- Most 11–16 year olds think that sex education should primarily come from parents, but admit that it actually comes from friends. Most parents believe that sex education should be done in schools, claiming that they are embarrassed or that their own sex education was inadequate.
- Most 16–21-year-old women think that their sex education was inadequate, concentrating too much on the mechanics and too little on moral/social aspects.

The World Health Organisation recently declared there to be no evidence that sex education leads to more or earlier sexual activity; it may well delay it.

Reflect

A lot of Christian young people end up torn between two worlds: on the one hand, they want to discover what God has to say about sex and sexuality, and to follow this advice; on the other, they are drawn toward the same behaviour as friends who aren't Christians.

Teenage sexual behaviour and standards are hardly mentioned in the Bible for two reasons:

1. There *were* no 'teenagers' as such during Bible times. At 13, with their Barmitzvah or Bathmitzvah, boys and girls became men and women.
2. Young people married early, often by arrangement and usually without prolonged or unchaperoned contact with their prospective spouse. This lack of contact made the possibility of having premarital sexual intercourse unlikely.

However, the Bible has a very healthy and strongly *positive* approach to human sexuality in general, most evident in the Song of Songs. The fact that this beautiful, erotic poem is even *in* the Bible should tell us something about God's approach to sex. It was written, not as an allegory of the relationship between God and his people, but as a celebration of God-given sexuality – of the love between a man and a woman. Sadly, we seem too often to have reversed the Bible's polarity, strong on inhibition but weak on telling people what's *right* with sex.

When Solomon addressed the matter of adultery, he was careful to give more encouragement and advice than prohibition. But as much as he warned his readers about the snares and entrapments of the adulteress, so he also praised the wise and virtuous woman:

Drink water from your own cistern, running water from your own well. Should your springs overflow in the streets, your streams of water in the public squares? Let them be yours alone, never to be shared with strangers. May your fountain be blessed, and may you rejoice in the wife of your youth. A loving doe, a graceful deer – may her breasts satisfy you always, may you ever be captivated by her love. (Proverbs 5:15–19)

We have suffered considerably from swallowing Greek culture in the early centuries after Christ. Many ancient Greek philosophers viewed sex as distasteful, an entrapment of the body from which they longed to be free. Plato would probably have agreed with comedian Stephen Fry's evaluation of sex as basically 'silly'.

Some medieval scholars (by whose time the priesthood had become firmly celibate) even thought that sex had been introduced with the Fall of Genesis 3. Before this, they argued, it had been unnecessary. The idea grew up that sex was essentially a sort of 'necessary evil', required to propagate the species, but really anything but savoury. Tony Campolo tells of his old youth leader's advice: 'Sex is dirty. Sex is disgusting. Sex is degrading. Save it for your wife!'

This is far from what Genesis tells us about God's understanding of sex. Rather than being a result of the Fall, sex and sexuality are included in what God declares to be 'very good' (Genesis 1:31) when creating woman and man.

> **'The later equation, "sex = sin",**
> **did not enter Christian history from**
> **the Hebrew scriptures,**
> **where sex is viewed as a gift of God.'**
>
> American Presbyterian theologian Robert McAfee Brown

Young people are aware that many of their parents and elders are cautious about sex. In fact many of us, especially in the Church, seem to be almost prudish in our understanding of it. It causes us embarrassment so that, by and large, we just don't talk about it. When was the last time you heard the Song of Songs being read in church, for instance, or a sermon being preached on sex? And because we don't talk about it, young people are rarely prepared for it.

Just before the French Revolution, a soldier called Pierre Choderlos de Laclos wrote a book which inflamed the polite, aristocratic society it described. Made recently into the film, *Dangerous Liaisons*, it's a moral tale told through immoral characters. One of them, having married young, has prided herself on her virtue. But although her marriage is considered faultless by society at large, it's without passion, and she lacks the emotional preparation to cope with the new feelings that beset her when she is seduced. Her sexual education has been more *don't*s than *do*s, and she is led by her prudishness and ignorance into committing adultery.

If we don't teach young people a positive, healthy approach to sexuality, then we risk leaving them similarly unprepared. It's not enough to tell them *not* to do something: we must tell them *why*. And telling them not to do something 'because we say so' is an even less compelling argument: for a teenager, being told by a parent *not* to do something is usually the single best reason for doing it. So if we really believe that casual sex isn't a good thing, we will have to think carefully why this is so, and find ways of explaining it to young people.

The Bible is very up-front about sexual matters. From Genesis to Revelation, the biblical writers pull no punches in their use of sexual metaphor, both for good and bad. Ezekiel 23 is so sexually explicit and lurid that, if it were ever read in church, it would most likely make the vicar blush! Somewhere along the line, we seem to have confused holiness with prudishness, and in so doing we have departed from a truly biblical approach. The Bible understands sex as an expression of love: but not only does it demonstrate the love that is there, it also enhances and deepens that love. This is why sex inevitably complicates relationships, a fact that most teenagers appreciate too late.

> **Sonia: 'Oh, don't Boris, please.**
> **Sex without love is an empty experience.'**
> **Boris: 'Yes, but as empty experiences go,**
> **it's one of the best.'**
>
> From Woody Allen's film, Love and Death

At a superficial level, casual sex affirms a person's sense of self-worth and attractiveness, and allows them to express the love they feel. Nowhere was this more evident than in the late 1960s, when love suddenly became 'free' and readily available. A generation sickened by violence, hatred and war, and inspired by naive idealism, threw off their parents' sexual repressions and tried to sow love by sowing their oats. We need to recognise the attractiveness of this approach to sex, which is still highly influential. But we also need to affirm, by adapting the words of the French philosopher Voltaire, that what society often views as good is actually the enemy of the best.

Casual sex teaches young people that love is temporary. But within the context of a strong and committed relationship, sex can be a lot more profound and meaningful without losing any of the fun. Because your partner loves you, and has promised to commit themselves to you unconditionally for life, you can share yourself with them at a much deeper level. Whilst the physical sensations are the same as in casual sex, sex within marriage can reinforce these feelings with far deeper emotions as well.

SEX

- Sex is healthy and God-given. It is not just a means of procreation, but is for our enjoyment and fulfilment.
- Since the Old Testament views body and soul as being inseparable, sex is a celebration of both body and soul.
- Like anything else in life, sex has rules of engagement, the violation of which lessens the experience.

Engage

The Church often seems to be morally outraged rather than compassionately concerned by teenage sex, an outrage born more of *self*-righteousness than of righteousness. Jesus' approach to sexual sin, seen in the episode of the woman caught in adultery (John 8:1–11), values compassion above condemnation. Ironically, the prophets, known for their condemnations, condemned nothing more forcefully than the absence of compassion. And in fact, we'll get much further with compassion and understanding than we will just by adamantly drawing a line in the sand.

> **'It's high time to recognise that sexual licence is not simply sinful, but rather, infinitely sad.'**
>
> John Smith, again

We seem to have our understanding of sin upside down. We must come to terms with the fact that *something is a sin because it's damaging and destructive, not damaging and destructive because it's a sin*. We must also learn how to present this argument to a generation often convinced that God is basically a killjoy.

It's important for us to realise that, like it or not, the majority of young people see nothing wrong with premarital sex. Whatever we think of it, if we deny this they will accuse us of not understanding them. And they will be right. It can often sound as if, having arbitrarily decided that something isn't allowed, we Christian adults are going to make absolutely sure that nobody enjoys it. The problem is that sin almost always seems appealing and enjoyable: after all, if it *didn't* seem appealing and enjoyable, there would be no temptation!

Sin is basically the abuse of something both good and God-given. Food, for instance, is good; feasts are more common than fasts in the Old Testament. But food addiction (gluttony) is bad. Rest is good, protected and prescribed in the Old Testament through the sabbath. But laziness is bad. Material assets are a blessing, but greed is a sin. So it is with sex: sex is good, but its abuse is destructive. However, the reason why sex *appears* to most people to be good in almost any context is that the appeal of the original remains even when it's been corrupted.

We need to ask ourselves 'Why does the Bible say something?' 'What's the rationale behind it?' It's not enough to tell young people, 'Don't!' We must explain to them why not. We must be prepared with reasons for our beliefs (cf. 1 Peter 3:15), and these reasons must make sense to young people. We must present sex in a positive, not prohibitive, way.

This becomes even more important if we are concerned, as we must be, with young people outside the Church. They aren't likely to be swayed by arguments which rely on God's authority, or by dogmatic declarations. But they may be open to well thought-out, reasoned advice which has their best interests at heart. Appealing to the intelligence and trust of teenagers will be more effective than appeals to our own sense of authority. We should be careful, however: if we're using sex education as a means to convert young people, they will probably reject both the advice and the evangelism.

Nor is it enough to present just one option in these complex times. Jesus presented marriage as final, but included a let-out clause for those whose marriages were already dead (Matt. 19:9).

Both he and Paul favoured lifelong celibacy, but included conces-
sions for those who would otherwise 'burn with passion' (1 Cor.
7:9). We have some precedents, therefore, for adopting multiple
solutions. We must present premarital abstinence as *the* model, and
help young people learn how to keep to this, teaching them how to
say 'No!'. But we must also teach young people about contracep-
tion, reducing the danger not only of getting each other pregnant,
but also of catching and spreading sexually-transmitted diseases
such as AIDS.

This may well be hard to swallow, since the last thing we want
to do is suggest to teenagers that sex outside marriage, as long as
they use a condom, is just fine and dandy! It's difficult to strike the
right balance. We don't want to tell young people that, if they don't
like the idea of keeping sex within marriage, they should just
ignore it and use a condom! And the fact is, of course, that even if
there were no risk of pregnancy or disease, premarital sex would
still not be too good an idea.

On the other hand, we don't want to fall into the irresponsible
trap of failing to inform young people about the full range of choices open to them, good and bad, simply because we're worried that
they will make the wrong one! God didn't say, in the Garden of
Eden, 'Well, I *would* tell you about the big tree in the middle of
the garden – the really obvious one with the knowledge of good
and evil, and the very attractive but lethal fruit – but I'm worried
that, if I do, you might be tempted to eat from it.'

The key is education: we need to equip young people to make
these decisions for themselves. If they're to make an informed
choice, for instance, young people will need to understand that
condoms make sex safer, *not* safe. They should know that:

- the Family Planning Association have estimated the failure rate
  of condoms to be up to 15 per cent when used by teenagers;
- the risk of pregnancy, or of contracting a sexually transmitted
  disease, without a condom is even higher;
- they are as much at risk from sexually transmitted diseases other
  than AIDS as from AIDS itself. These include herpes, syphilis,
  chancroid, pelvic inflammatory disease, gonorrhoea, warts and
  genital chlamydia.

A healthy youth group programme, and a healthy preaching calendar, should include both teaching and discussion on sex – down to earth and practical rather than dogma which does nothing more than condemn and induce guilt. We should make it clear that the gospel affects and concerns every part of our lives, not just the 'spiritual', and that God cares for our physical, moral, social, intellectual, medical, psychological and sexual well-being.

Any contact that isn't superficial with the young people in your area, whether they are Christian or not, will reveal that a lot of this teaching will come 'too late'. It's therefore important to teach young people about forgiveness: God's, ours and their own. Guilt is a strong emotion in young people, often regardless of whether or not they have done something worthy of it. Forgiveness and renewal are basic Christian principles that we *must* teach our children. Unconditional love, an overwhelmingly *positive* message, is the essence of the gospel. We mustn't allow ourselves to be sidetracked into 'guiltmongering'.

What should we do?

1. Seek to understand what young people actually think about sex and sexuality.
2. Understand that many young people have been hurt sexually: through abuse, rape, neglect, etc. Others have been hurt in other ways, but express this hurt sexually, often through being promiscuous.
3. Engage in *serious* thinking about why God says that sex is best within marriage, and discover *effective* means of conveying this to teenagers.

How should we do this?

- Develop a healthy *youth group programme* for discussing sex and sexuality. Look at positive ways in which we can influence and encourage young people. There is a mountain of resources available for this from bookshops and organisations dealing with teenage sexuality. Above all, it's important to create an environment in which young people feel that they can discuss sex without embarrassment or fear of ridicule.
- Supplement sex education in schools and elsewhere by *teaching*

about sex to pre-adolescents. We tell children that Noah took the animals into the ark two by two, but we never tell them why! Too often, we talk about sex to young people only when they are 16, by which time half of them are already veterans!

- Parents have input into their children's *school sex education* through the governors and through teachers. Resources such as *Make Love Last* are available specifically for this purpose. Teachers may be grateful for parental input and support, especially in view of the fact that most children want sex education to come primarily from their parents.

- Since prevention is better than cure, we might establish *parent seminars,* or *breakfasts* or *coffee mornings* for mums and dads, both as resources and for teaching. Though most young people want to learn about sex from their parents rather than from other sources, such as the media or their friends, research shows that this is not happening. We must help parents overcome their own feelings of embarrassment, inadequacy and guilt, showing them how to communicate to their children, as well as explaining why this is so important.

Although this chapter has dealt predominantly with teenage sex, we should note in conclusion that *sexuality is about a lot more than just sex*: it is about being fully human. What we teach young people about sex and sexuality, therefore, is what we teach them about life, and about being human. Sexuality is part of identity, part of who we are.

Further information

Agencies

Christian Initiative on Teenage Sexuality assists church and youth leaders to teach God's truth about sex and sexuality, through leader training days, newsletters, resources and statistical information. Contact Anne Carlos via Care for the Family.

Books

Steve Chalke and Nick Page, *Sex Matters* (Hodder & Stoughton, 1996).

Joyce Huggett, *Life in a Sex-Mad Society* (IVP, 1988).
John White, *Eros Defiled* (IVP, 1979).

Videos

Make Love Last, a video used in almost one-third of secondary schools, teaches abstinence as the most effective contraceptive. It is available from Care for the Family, 53 Romney Street, London SWlP 3RF. Tel: 0171-233 0455.

Lessons In Love, seven 15-minute talks on sex and relationships for specifically Christian young people, a video I did with Care for the Family.

Chapter 3

Homelessness

A COUPLE OF YEARS AGO, I was filming with GMTV near London's King's Cross Station. I met a girl there I shall call Lisa, who was 13 years old and sleeping rough. She had run away from care when she was abused, only to be raped on the streets. Her mother was in a rehabilitation clinic for help to get her off addiction to heroin. Lisa had started on soft drugs and sniffing glue. The police were aware of her situation, but nothing changed. 'All I want is to be back home,' she told me.

Many homeless people would echo these sentiments.

Listen

The reasons why people end up homeless are many and complex. Shelter, a charity especially concerned with homeless people, simplifies it all down to one principle: there isn't enough affordable housing. But this is perhaps a little too simple. In reality, homelessness is a much more tricky issue, full of grey areas. We delude ourselves if we think that simply building houses will solve the problem; however, it will go a long way.

Lack of affordable housing is a major factor in the homelessness statistics. According to Department of the Environment figures, between 1975 and 1990 the total number of new houses built per annum dropped by two-thirds. The number of houses built by private investment rose by almost one-third, whilst the number of public sector new houses (including those built by housing associations) declined by over 90 per cent. In other words, fewer houses are being built, and the majority of those that are built are for purchase or private rental.

The Thatcher government's policy of selling off council houses to their owners at cut price was an excellent idea in theory, and was definitely good news for some of those individuals who bought their council houses. But in practice, the policy has shown itself to be merely another symptom of a philosophy that values the good of the individual at the expense of the greater common good. Local councils, unable to replenish their housing stock in spite of continued demand, have found themselves struggling to house all those people they're legally obliged to provide homes for. Many have had to resort to putting individuals and families temporarily into bed and breakfast accommodation, since the cost of private renting is often too high.

After the last recession and the various rises in interest rates, many people who did purchase their council houses then found themselves unable to keep up the mortgage repayments. People who had secure jobs when they arranged their mortgage found themselves suddenly unemployed and in arrears.

According to Shelter, 58,540 properties were repossessed in England in 1993. Some other organisations put this figure even higher, at 60,500. At the end of 1993, some 316,430 home owners were six months or more behind with their mortgage repayments. Although this was a decline from the peak in 1991, rent and mortgage arrears still accounted for about 10 per cent of all homelessness.

But homelessness isn't just a city problem: it's a nationwide problem. In fact, almost one-third of all homeless people live outside big cities. The increase in commuting has pushed middle income families further out into the countryside than ever, and has led in part to the increase of homelessness in rural areas. People in lower income families, in the small towns in which they have lived all their lives, might find themselves unable to buy or rent a house within their means, since middle income families are buying up the available property or renting at a higher cost. Some families find that their landlord wants to sell the property, and they become homeless when they can't find another affordable place in which to live.

**'You can qualify as "homeless" by
convincing the local authority that you are
unintentionally homeless;
that you are a priority need,
with dependent children, pregnant or vulnerable;
and that you are without a roof.
If you fail to qualify as "homeless",
you can join a council house waiting list.
About 1.5 million people are already waiting.'**

Rachel Kelly in The Times, 30th March 1994

Changes in social security legislation in recent years have added significantly to the number of homeless young people. Since September 1988, the majority of 16–17 year olds have been excluded from claiming income support. Although places on training schemes are guaranteed by the government for those not in school or employment, the reality is that a great many young people have fallen through the net. Training scheme placements have not always been available, and many of those that exist are substandard, causing bored and disillusioned teenagers to leave. The Labour Force Survey for the winter of 1993–94 estimated there to be about 90,000 16–17 year olds with no discernible income.

It's reckoned that somewhere in the region of 30–40 per cent of people living on the streets have some degree of mental illness. The closure of 23,000 psychiatric hospital beds during the 1980s led to a great increase in the levels of homeless people with mental health problems. Closures were due partly to the increased financial constraints placed on the National Health Service by 'streamlining' and the so-called 'internal market', and partly to the policy of 'care in the community'.

It is difficult to find a professional working in the fields of mental health or social work who disagrees with the principle of 'care in the community', and in some well-resourced areas, it is no doubt working well. But all too often, the constraints placed on community care providers by the lack of funding and general resources have hindered its effective implementation.

In a recent survey of 110 homeless young people in Southwark, central London, over 50 per cent said that they had left home because of an argument with a relative. This is not as easily patched up as you might think. Step-parents are a frequent cause of conflict. If a child and step-parent come to resent one another, the child can end up leaving home in the belief that anything is better than their present situation. Sometimes a rift between child and step-parent can force the remaining parent to choose between them.

Some children are forced to leave home, either because there aren't enough funds to support them, or because their parent or parents don't know how to deal with their behaviour. Others leave because they can no longer endure the abuse they have suffered at home.

According to the London Research Centre, roughly 35 per cent of households accepted as homeless in London are single-parent households (the majority of whom are single mothers). Many single mothers want to work in order to avoid the trap of homelessness and poverty, but find that their efforts are hampered by the costs of employing a registered childminder to look after the children while they are out. Single mothers often lack the qualifications, experience and confidence needed to get a job that pays highly enough.

But the break up of the family is not only a major factor in *causing* homelessness: it's also one of its inevitable *consequences*. The loss of contact with relations can be psychologically very destructive, adding to the sense of isolation and the lack of self-respect already felt by homeless people.

The destructive role played by family fragmentation is shown by the alarming number of homeless young people who have been, at some point in their lives, in the care of local authorities. The most vulnerable young people often end up in care, and local authorities are always stretched to meet their needs. It's estimated that 70 per cent of the 'rent boys' around London's Leicester Square, and 55 per cent of the prostitutes around King's Cross, have been in care at one time or another. Many young people leave care at the earliest opportunity, when they reach age 16. They are attracted by the prospect of freedom and independence, only to find themselves out on the street.

> **'Care leavers are vastly over-represented in the homelessness statistics.**
> **Fewer than I per cent of people under 18 are in care, yet up to 40 per cent of young people who end up on the streets have been in care.'**
>
> Sarah Knibbs, Community Care magazine

Sleeping rough is the tip of an iceberg that includes squats, bed and breakfast, hostels, caravans and other forms of temporary accommodation. But once a person is on the streets, they are open to all sorts of problems, dangers and complications. For instance, homeless people are 150 times more likely than others to contract TB, and considerably less able to recover once they have it. Homeless women and girls have a greater susceptibility to rape, and some find that prostitution is the only way off the streets. To kill the boredom and depression, many homeless people turn to alcohol and drugs, only to get hooked. (Of course, it may have been alcohol or drug abuse which pushed them onto the streets in the first place.)

Most homeless people desperately want to leave the streets or their temporary accommodation and move into 'real' homes. But this can be extremely difficult. Many find themselves embroiled in a 'Catch-22' scenario. In order to afford somewhere to live, they need money; in order to get money, they need a job; but in order to find a job they need somewhere to live. Employers don't look too kindly on hiring people with 'no fixed abode', or even with a hostel address. And without a job, it's almost impossible to afford decent housing, either to rent or to buy.

According to Shelter:

- Local councils throughout England accepted 127,290 households – which represents perhaps as many as 365,000 individuals – as officially homeless in 1994. They registered 61,120 households in the first half of 1995 (a fall of nearly 5 per cent on the first half of 1994).
- There are about 77,000 single homeless people in London alone.

- Around 60 per cent of those sleeping rough (the 1991 Census figure for rough sleepers, which should be considered a minimum, was 2,674 people) are outside London. 77 per cent of homeless households in 1994 were outside London.
- At the end of June 1995, 4,830 households (perhaps as many as 13,860 individuals, including an estimated 5,500 children) were living in bed and breakfast accommodation in England, and 45,750 families were in temporary accommodation.
- The cost of building a new home to rent is around £8,000, compared with about £11,600 to keep a family in bed and breakfast for a year.
- 49,210 properties in England were repossessed during 1994 (a fall of 16 per cent from 1993). At the end of 1994, 419,890 people were behind in their mortgage repayments by three months or more.
- Just under half of those accepted as homeless by London authorities belong to ethnic minorities.
- During 1994, roughly 6,960 households were accepted as being homeless because one member was diagnosed as being mentally ill.

According to Barnardo's:

- In 1991, 45 per cent of 16 and 17 year olds claiming 'severe hardship' benefits had slept rough at some point. 25 per cent had had to beg, steal or sell drugs to survive. 25 per cent had criminal convictions, and 25 per cent of the girls were pregnant. Two-thirds of those not living at home had been thrown out, and 20 per cent said that they had been sexually or physically abused while at home. In 1991, 76,957 people aged 16 or 17 claimed 'severe hardship' benefit.

According to London's Centrepoint:

- About 29 per cent of those they deal with have been in care. 38 per cent of these in 1993 were aged 16–17, compared with 10 per cent in 1979.
- About 37 per cent of London borough housing departments

have insufficient housing for those leaving care. 65 per cent are using bed and breakfast for care leavers.

• Nearly 40 per cent of those seen by Centrepoint had entered care because of family arguments; 15 per cent had been told to leave home by parents; 11 per cent had left after having been sexually or physically abused; only 13 per cent had left home to look for work or independence.

Reflect

Contrary, perhaps, to expectations, homelessness and its equivalents *do* exist in the Bible: in fact, homelessness occurs as early as Genesis 4. Having done away with his brother Abel in a fit of jealousy, Cain is cursed to wander the earth restlessly. Eden will no longer provide for him. He is, to all intents and purposes, made homeless. The dramatic consequence of this action for Cain is that he and his kin are excluded from the official genealogy. In other words, being homeless means more than having nowhere to live: it means having no place in the community. It means being an outcast.

The initial history of the Israelite people is one of homelessness. They were nomadic until Joseph, and following the exodus the Israelites had nowhere to live. The transition between servitude in Egypt and a home in Canaan was so traumatic that many lost their faith, while others wished for the abuse they had suffered at the hands of Pharaoh rather than the displacement of exile. The Promised Land was more than just a place to live: it was somewhere to call their own, somewhere which could define their identity.

> **'The Jews deserve a homeland,**
> **not because they are Jews,**
> **but because they are human.'**
>
> Palestinian Elias Chacour

In the Old Testament, society was structured in a very particular way: every adult male had a profession, almost always that of his father. Every daughter was brought up to be married and to carry out the duties of wife, mother, cook and housekeeper. Every family had land. A woman was considered to be under the protection of her father until she married, when she came under the protection of her husband. A boy would remain in his father's house until marriage, and sometimes afterwards. His father would equip him with a trade, which would always stand him in good stead. Theoretically, all bases were covered.

There were, however, people who fell through the net. If a child was disabled, he or she was considered unable to carry out useful work. If their family was unable or unwilling to look after them, they would seek support from the public. Every city had beggars at its gate, and every beggar was considered in some way to be unable to contribute, to be an outcast. In Mosaic law, some forms of disability and illness (such as leprosy) left a person ritually unclean, in which case they were kept isolated. This often meant that they were homeless.

In addition to this, if a woman left her father's house to marry, and her husband then died, it was up to one of her husband's brothers to marry and take care of her (cf. Matt. 22:23–33). If her late husband's brothers were for some reason unwilling or unable to do this, she would return to the house of her father. If this wasn't possible, she would be forced to beg alms or else resort to prostitution in order to feed and clothe herself and her children. Ruth chose to go with her mother-in-law, even though this meant being homeless and left to beg for food, when her husband and father-in-law both died (see Ruth 2 and Deuteronomy 24:19). She was saved from destitution only by her relative Boaz.

The prophets were extremely concerned about the plight of widows and orphans – those without any financial support. Isaiah's exhortation to Israel to 'defend the cause of the fatherless and plead the case of the widow' (1:17; cf. 10:2) is by no means peculiar. It's found explicitly in Jeremiah (7:6; 22:3), Ezekiel (22:7), Zechariah (7:10) and Malachi (3:5), and implicitly throughout the Old Testament. In the New Testament, this theme is reprised by James (1:27).

Micah condemns outright those who defraud others of their houses (2:2). And Isaiah (58:7) explicitly lists the provision of 'the poor wanderer with shelter' among the elements to be observed as part of 'the true fast'.

David became homeless when he was exiled by his own son. He wrote in Psalm 68 that God was a 'father to the fatherless, a defender of widows', who 'houses the isolated'. (To the Old Testament way of thinking, a house was a household: not simply bricks and mortar to keep the rain off one's head, but a person's family, their place in society.) A later psalmist takes this up again in Psalm 146.

> **'Home is the place where,**
> **when you have to go there,**
> **they have to take you in.'**
>
> US poet Robert Frost

Jesus broke all taboos by talking and associating with outcasts. In Matthew 8, he even numbers himself among the homeless. (Matthew 2:13–15 reminds us that Jesus was a 'displaced person' as a child.) But Matthew 25 makes it abundantly clear that homelessness is no virtue: the word normally translated 'stranger' in the parable of the sheep and the goats could be translated 'exile' or 'alien': a homeless person in a foreign land. And the description of 'the least' (or 'insignificants') covers many of the worst problems associated with homelessness: hunger, thirst, shelter, clothing, health care, companionship and justice.

The early Church viewed social provision as integral to the gospel. Acts 4 describes the perfect community, in which people became voluntarily homeless in the full assurance that their fellow-Christians would look after them. In Acts 6, the Church elected seven men to cope with material provision for widows and orphans. The early Church placed great emphasis on community, something our modern churches seem all too often to have lost. Things were held in common so that nobody was in need: the early Church provided a community in which members cared for one another in very tangible ways. More than this, because it was a missionary community, this care was extended to those beyond it.

All this makes homelessness very much an issue which the Church needs to address once more.

HOMELESSNESS

- Homelessness is the loss of a person's place in society, and an indication of the value placed upon a person by that society. To become homeless is to become an outcast.
- Jesus sided himself firmly with the outcasts, shunning society in favour of reaching out to those who needed help (cf. Phil. 2:6).
- Jesus considered that Christians would be known by their fruit, by the way they treated the 'insignificants' of society. The Church has a commitment to care for those without the where-withal to care for themselves, showing a preferential option for the 'insignificants'.

Engage

We may be tempted to think that the most immediate thing we can do is give money to homeless people. Then at least we feel we are doing something, even if they subsequently spend the money on the wrong things. Actually, however, homelessness is a *structural* problem, and it requires a *structural* answer. Your money can be used more effectively by organisations which tackle the problem at this structural level.

Your church could do a local audit, discovering if there is a problem locally with homelessness, even if there are few homeless people where you are. After all, homeless people usually come from somewhere other than where they end up. It may be that your area *makes* people homeless, rather than receiving them. Homelessness is not just a big-city problem; it is increasing in rural areas at an alarming rate.

The advantage of an audit is that it aims to discover *why* people are homeless, as well as the scale of the problem locally. It's important to try and stop people becoming homeless, rather than simply helping them back into society once they *are* homeless. We have already seen the reasons why people, young people especially, generally become homeless. Your audit will probably reveal this pattern, but it will give you specific *local* information, which you will need to form specifically *local* solutions. Once you know why people become homeless in your area, you will be better equipped to combat homelessness at the root level.

It's also a good idea to take a careful audit of your church. Homelessness projects cost money and need high levels of staffing: if the resources and commitment you need don't exist in your church, you may find it useful to collaborate with other local churches or organisations. It is important to estimate *realistically* what you can afford and what you can provide (cf. Luke 14:28–33), and the level of support you can expect from your church. (You will need this support in order to cope with the disappointments which are sure to come.)

It is vital that you know what you are doing. If you are serious about setting up a project, you should inform yourself and your church about every aspect of housing and homelessness, both nationally and locally. You should also be aware of what provisions exist near you for homeless people. It's no good setting up a crisis centre if the real need in your area is for intermediate housing. Lots of churches do a soup run on a Saturday night, and there are one or two places in London where the homeless can't move for a sea of congealed soup. Don't try to fill a gap which doesn't exist.

'Do try this at home . . .'

If you feel that your church, or group of churches, is able to set up a specific project, the first thing to do is to contact the local authority housing department. They may well prove initially sceptical, so you will have to assure them first that your intention is to help, not convert, the homeless; and second, that you are going into this with your eyes open. It might create bad feeling if you were to present the local council with a *fait accompli*. Because of regulations and financial constraints, local councils often need independent ventures to cope with the problem, so it is important not to sour your welcome.

Oasis Trust

Since its beginning, the organisation I work for, the Oasis Trust, has been involved with homeless people. Working in partnership with other organisations, including the Aluddan Homes Housing

Association, we run various projects in inner-city London, all of which could be duplicated elsewhere in the country.

- *Intermediate housing:* in February 1990, five years after work started on the project, Oasis opened No. 3, a referred-access, medium-stay hostel in Peckham. This caters for ten people aged between 16 and 25. Permanent staff and volunteers assess the long-term housing needs of the residents, teaching them the necessary skills for independent living, and planning with them how to get permanent accommodation. The emphasis is on training and encouragement, equipping residents to stand on their own two feet. Staff help residents to find jobs, or places on training schemes or college courses, and encourage them to develop trusting relationships with other people. No. 3 is careful about who it accepts: it does not, for instance, cater for those with mental health, drug or alcohol related problems, because there aren't specialist staff in these areas. It's important not to bite off more than you can chew: do what you can and do it well.

- *Move-on Accommodation:* in 1992, Oasis was approached by a Streatham church about working together on a housing project for homeless young people. We purchased a three-storey house, divided into eight bedsit apartments suitable for young people leaving hostel accommodation. No. 24 opened officially in 1995. Residents are used to an element of independent living, but a site worker provides advice and support whenever it's needed, and a communal lounge limits the isolation that bedsits otherwise produce.

- *Health care:* the Elizabeth Baxter Health Centre, near Waterloo Station, caters for the health care needs of London's homeless people. 'Lizzies' is a drop-in centre providing everything from chiropody and nursing to a hot drink and a listening ear. It is considered by many homeless people to have 'the best showers in town'. A consultant psychiatrist from Guy's Hospital runs regular clinics for those with mental health problems. Above all, the staff at 'Lizzies' treat the homeless with the dignity and respect they may not receive elsewhere. Lizzies was started to fill a big gap in the market, and runs in partnership with the statutory authorities.

- *The mobile care unit and street teams:* each team goes out on the same night weekly, with the same personnel, to the same area, for the same reason: to spend time with homeless people, building relationships which may well become a bridge to some form of help or accommodation. Consistency is vital. Team members are volunteers, who receive regular training and are prepared to offer advice as well as friendship, if needed. They are supported by the mobile care unit, a specially converted double-decker bus offering not only an alternative place to talk but also hot drinks, information about other agencies and a mobile phone to help find accommodation.

The Shaftesbury Society

Oasis is far from being the only Christian organisation involved in this type of work. The Shaftesbury Society, for instance, is also deeply involved in housing and hostels, especially for those in the 16–26 age bracket. Their many projects include:

- Two *direct access hostels,* taking people straight from the streets. In the course of a year, 450 young men and women stay in one of these, receiving not only a roof over their heads, but also help in finding longer-term accommodation and jobs.
- *Lena Fox House,* the next stage on, a 44-bed, low-rent residence in Bermondsey. It offers long-term accommodation in a variety of formats, with differing amounts of support: from single rooms with shared facilities, bedsits with their own cooking facilities, to shared or single flats for those able to cope fully with independent living, until residents can find something on their own.
- *A rent/deposit scheme* in Merton, South London, helping homeless people get private accommodation by providing the up-front deposit and six months' rent guaranteed. The scheme vets landlords and properties to make sure that tenants are being offered a fair deal, helps them get whatever state benefits they're entitled to, and represents their interests when the landlord is clearly in breach of contract. But it also helps landlords by vetting potential tenants to make sure that they're suitable, and by putting good business their way.

- *A resources centre*, helping people who have been homeless, and are moving into more permanent accommodation, to find the furniture and trappings essential for making a place habitable.
- *Church-linked community initiatives*, something the society has been involved in in one way or another for over 150 years. Usually run in partnership with local groups or the local authority, they aim to provide for the needs of homeless people, helping them to resettle into the wider community.
- *A partnership scheme and a consultancy service*, helping churches set up and maintain high quality care and support initiatives for the local area.

Further information

Organisations

Shelter, 88 Old Street, London EC1V 9HU. Tel: 0171-253 0202.

UNLEASH, Trinity House, 4 Chapel Court, Borough High Street, London SE1 1HN. Tel: 0171-735 2166.

CHAR (Campaign for Single Homeless), 5–15 Cromer Street, London WC1H 8LS. Tel: 0171-833 2071.

CNHC (Churches National Housing Coalition), Central Buildings, Oldham Street, Manchester M1 1JT. Tel: 0161-236 9321.

Shaftesbury Society, 16 Kingston Road, London SW19 1JZ. Tel: 0181-542 5550.

Oasis Trust, 87 Blackfriars Road, London SE1 8HA. Tel: 0171-928 9422.

Books

Fran Beckett, *Called to Action* (Fount, 1989).

London Hostels Directory, from the Resource Information Service, 5 Egmont House, 116 Shaftesbury Avenue, London W1V 7DJ.

Chapter 4

Parenting

THE FAMILY HAS ALWAYS been the basic unit of society: not merely Western society, but almost every society around the world. Yet 'traditional family values' are being eroded. Marriage as a life-long commitment has never been so unpopular. Divorce is at an all-time high, and nearly a fifth of all family units involve single parents.

Children are under tremendous pressure from all sides. Almost half of all reported crime is now reckoned to be committed by young people, and recent research has linked this with a lack of parental love and security. All this means that the issue of parenting is a critical one for every local church.

Listen

'It's twins! No . . . sorry . . . this one's the training manual!' This is something never heard in the hospital delivery room. First-time parents, anxious that everything should be perfect – and as yet unaware that everything can *never* be perfect – can find the rude awakening to parenthood difficult to bear. And it doesn't get easier!

As Kierkegaard once said, life has to be lived forwards, even though it can only be understood backwards. In other words, like everyone else, parents have to act without the benefit of hindsight. And with the unpredictability of different children, each with constantly-developing personalities and changing requirements, this is no easy task. Parenting for each child means steering uncharted waters. And we only get one shot. Even if we have several children, few of us will parent a child to 18 before we begin again, so we never get a chance to see the 'finished product', and learn from our mistakes with the next child.

The first challenge for every new mother is merely to survive the traumas of pregnancy – the nausea, the discomfort, the frustration, the backpains, the swelling, the cravings, the body changes, the feelings of unattractiveness, the inability to sleep, etc. But if this disruption seems bad, it is nothing compared to the birth of a child.

Even if new parents have prepared themselves for the arrival of a child, they rarely can prepare themselves adequately for the changes which inevitably, and quite often dramatically, occur in their own relationship. Practically and emotionally, a couple is changed for ever once they become parents, and it can be quite difficult to come to terms with this change. In spite of their desire for a child, parents can still grieve for the loss of their independence.

> **'Almost conspiratorially we compared
> our feelings of guilt.
> Yet we hated being trapped in
> a working environment which prevented us from
> spending more time with our children:
> not just time that we would like to spend with
> them, but time that we fear they need from us.'**
>
> Mary Ann Sieghart, The Times, 11th April 1994

The pressures of modern life mean that most of us live at high speed. Benjamin Franklin quipped that 'time is money', but in fact time is much more valuable than money. What children need most from their parents before school age is time. They need the absolute assurance that they are loved, and they measure this in the amount and quality of the attention they're given. It can be extremely hard for busy parents to find this time, especially if they work. But, as the saying goes, no one ever confessed on their deathbed that they wished they'd spent more time at the office!

School, when it comes, can be interesting or boring for children. This depends, to a large extent, on whether they perceive education as an exciting adventure or a dreaded chore. And this, in turn, depends a lot on their initial, pre-school experience with learning. If their parents have managed to make learning seem fun and relevant, then some of this same enthusiasm will remain with children during their school years. If not, there is a danger that children will do little more than is required of them by their teachers. Their education, which forms much of their preparation for life, will be more passive than active; and this can have big consequences for them in the future.

> **'The secret of happy children lies in a child's preschool years. It is the love and input a child receives during these crucial five years which will define the nature of the adult. . . . It is confidence which makes children happy. Those who feel good about themselves know they can tackle things and succeed. But, just as importantly, a confident child will find it easier to cope when things in life don't go according to plan.'**
>
> Childminder Susan Warren, Daily Express,
> 31st August and 1st September 1994

Discipline and authority are minefields for the modern parent. Whether or not it is right to smack children is a big issue. Government guidelines issued by Virginia Bottomley, when she was Health Secretary, gave childminders the right to smack their charges provided the parents gave their consent. This caused concern in some sections of society. According to one large and vocal group, smacking is a blatant form of violence which is both immoral and prone to teach children that violence is an acceptable response. But set against this is the general assumption that, however much a parent may dislike doing it, smacking is the only stern form of saying 'No!' that a two year old understands.

As children grow into adolescence, slowly granting them independence at the same time as maintaining a framework of discipline involves striking a difficult balance. They are likely to take whatever independence they're not given, but they still need to know that their parents love and care for them. And many children, even if only subconsciously, still recognise the limits parents place on their behaviour to be indications of their love and concern – however wrong they may also consider them to be!

'Possessive parents rarely live long enough to see the fruits of their selfishness.'

Novelist Alan Garner

As they mature, children grow closer to their peers than their parents. Although this has probably always been the case, the gap between friends and parents has widened considerably in the last fifty years. Between the time my parents were born and the time I was born, for instance, the worlds of parenting and childhood changed almost beyond recognition. A minister I once met visiting a church in the Midlands summed up the old order of things when he told me, 'When I was 15, all I wanted was to be like my dad, and to have a suit like his.' By the time *I* was 15, the *last* thing any teenager wanted was a suit like their father's!

With society changing so fast, it can be hard to understand the world in which children live. A few years ago, a High Court judge made the headlines by admitting, in the middle of a case, that he had no idea who Madonna was. But if some parents reading this are scratching their heads, tempted to confess the same level of ignorance, they should understand that Madonna was yesterday's idol. And the rock bands and film stars whose pictures currently line the walls of numerous teenagers' bedrooms will probably be out of fashion even by the time this book is published. Nevertheless, although catching up with your children's fast-moving culture may seem like an impossible task, it can demonstrate to your child that you are interested in them.

The Observer estimated in June 1991 that 90 per cent of British people marry at some point in their lives, but that 37 per cent of these marriages end in divorce. Figures have risen from 477 divorces in 1901, to 58,239 in 1970, to 165,000 in 1990. According to a survey published in *The Guardian* in September 1991, almost one in five families is now headed by a lone parent. The Office of

Population, Censuses and Surveys records a rise in one-parent families from 8 per cent in 1971 to 19 per cent in 1991.

This fragmentation of the family should worry us. Many lone parents bring up their children with more love and security than some other more traditional families. But most people still agree that the ideal situation is to have children brought up in a loving, secure, stable environment with both the mother and the father present.

In his book *Why Wait?*, Josh McDowell reports the findings of a John Hopkins University study, that 'young white teenage girls living in fatherless families . . . were 60 per cent more likely to have premarital intercourse than those living in two-parent homes'. The Joseph Rowntree Foundation recently backed up these findings with a study of their own, suggesting – strongly against received social wisdom – that 'staying together for the children' *is* in general better for the children than ending a marriage in divorce.

Care for the Family director Rob Parsons explains the trend: 'A lack of self-worth is behind so many of the ills which plague our society today. It leads many teenagers into a promiscuous lifestyle that is so often motivated not by the search for sex, but by a longing to be wanted.'

As a result of this trend, every year over 8,000 girls under the age of 16 become pregnant. They usually lack a secure partner, secure housing, employment, finance and emotional support. Being a parent is tough enough when you have these things: without them it is considerably harder, which makes it all the more likely that this vicious circle will continue.

The disintegration of the family unit, however, has a much greater impact than simply on children. Because they are the building blocks of society, like the individual cells of a biological organism, the break-up of the family threatens to tear the very fabric of society into little pieces. If this seems a bit melodramatic, we would do well to remember the analysis of Edward Gibbon in *The Decline and Fall of the Roman Empire*: that Rome effectively imploded: self-destructed. It became vulnerable to conquest by the Barbarians only because its internal fabric was already shot to pieces.

Singapore has become so concerned about the destruction of its traditional family values, the lynchpin of its society, that it has not only mounted a huge advertising campaign to promote the idea of the traditional family, but is also considering legislation to rein-force this campaign. Chief Rabbi Jonathan Sacks, in an article in *The Times* (28th August 1993), sounded a severe warning to our society: 'The question today is not whether we can create some-thing larger than the nuclear family, but whether we can survive something smaller and less stable.'

According to the Office of Population, Censuses and Surveys:

• In 1971, 8 per cent of families with dependent children were sin-gle-parent families. In 1991 this had risen to 19 per cent.

According to a 1994 report by the Joseph Rowntree Foundation:

• Girls under 16 living with step-parents are twice as likely as those living with both parents to give birth still in their teens and/or out of wedlock; three times as likely to leave home because of family arguments; and four times as likely to marry before the age of 20.
• Children whose parents are divorced are twice as likely to leave school at 16 as those living with both parents.

According to a survey done by the Christian Research Associa-tion, published in *The Times*, 19th June 1991:

• The average father spends twenty-five minutes per week (three-and-a-half minutes per day) in genuine conversation with their child or children. The average mother spends thirty-eight min-utes per week (five-and-a-half minutes per day). Yet the aver-age child spends twenty-one *hours* per week (three hours per day) watching television.

Reflect

Although we frequently forget this when approaching the issue of Christianity and the family, the biblical writers did not know and would not have appreciated the 'nuclear family': mum, dad and the kids. For people in the Bible, 'family' was a whole lot bigger. At the time of Abraham, for instance, the family as headed by a patriarch would include his wife (or wives) and concubines, his sons, their wives and concubines, *their* sons and unmarried daughters, everyone's servants, and any widows and aliens picked up along the way. This does not, of course, take account of the livestock!

By the time of Jesus, monogamy was more common than polygamy, concubines were uncommon, and servants were only for the wealthy. However, families still lived together in extended units of up to five generations, as they do even today in many parts of Africa, the East and the Middle East.

Although the task of parenting is considered in Genesis to have a divine mandate – the famous 'go forth and multiply' of Genesis 9:7 – people were warned after the Fall that rearing children was going to be an uphill struggle. The world into which they would be born was not a perfect place in which to live, and would cause anguish to parents who loved their children. Genesis 3:16 and Matthew 24:19 both allude to the hopelessness of bringing children into the world, a hopelessness we often hear echoed today.

Families did not start off well in the Bible. The first family came to a crashing end when Cain killed Abel in a fit of jealousy. Nor did things get much better after that: Ham shamed his drunken father, Noah; Jacob stole his brother Esau's birthright; Joseph annoyed his brothers so much that they sold him into slavery; Eli's sons were so corrupt and beyond his control that God cut them down on the same day, the news of which killed their father; Saul's crimes and misdemeanours led to the death of his three sons.

David's children fared no better, with Amnon raping his half-sister Tamar before being killed by his half-brother Absalom (whose name, ironically, means 'Father of Peace'). Absalom, in turn, died staging a *coup d'état* against his father, David. Solomon's family was so large that the book of Kings doesn't even try to list it all, but his two eldest sons split Israel in two, an action which ultimately contributed to the demise of the whole nation.

But this rather depressing catalogue of disasters is *specifically reversed* by Paul in 1 Timothy 2:15. He argues that Christ, in saving all creation, has made the world a *good* place into which to bring children.

Although we tend to think of it as a predominantly Christian idea, the family as the centre of the faith is quite distinctly Jewish.

The family, for instance, was where Jews were instructed to celebrate the important festival of Passover (Exodus 12). But one of the many radical reinterpretations of Judaism performed by Jesus was his extension of the notion of family to include the entire Church. When he was told that his mother and brothers had come to see him in Galilee (Matt. 12:46–50), Jesus asked his hearers, 'Who is my mother, and who are my brothers?' This was not so much a snub of his blood relatives as an inclusion of all his followers under the title of 'family'.

> **'Children have never been very good at listening to their elders, but they have never failed to imitate them.'**
>
> American novelist James Baldwin

That this notion of family was taken to heart by the disciples is evident from the insistence in 1 John that all are brothers. Paul similarly exhorts Timothy to treat older members of the Ephesian church as parents and younger members as children (1 Tim. 5:1–2). Paul seems to have considered Timothy like a son to him, and we can only assume that Timothy considered Paul to be like a father. This echoes 2 Kings 2:12, in which Elisha sees Elijah in the role of a father.

The ultimate father-figure, of course, is God. Again, we tend to associate this idea with Jesus when it's actually Jewish. In Deuteronomy 1:31, God is said to be 'like a father'. But he is referred to *specifically* as 'Father' in Psalm 2:7, Psalm 89:26, Isaiah 63:16 and 64:8, Jeremiah 3:4, 19, and in Malachi 2:10. The father image of God is alluded to particularly strongly when Isaiah's own children are used as a sign of the worsening relationship between God and his people (Isaiah 7–9).

What is surprising for us, perhaps, is the revelation in Isaiah 49:15 and 66:13 that God's love is also like that of a mother. The father image of God, given pride of place because of the particular relationship between Jesus and God, is never considered to be exclusive. What is significant is that the almighty God is referred to as a *parent*.

Jesus' own relationship with God sets the tone for our family relationships. Jesus called God 'Abba', a term both of respect and great intimacy. And although only Mark (14:36) refers to this explicitly, we can reasonably assume that it's the image Jesus had in mind whenever he called God 'Father', such as in the Lord's Prayer. In Romans 8:15 and Galatians 4:6, Paul tells us that we have been given 'a Spirit of adoption', and that it's this Spirit which makes us recognise God as *Abba*.

God set the example of parenthood in the Bible as involving a relationship of respect and intimacy. It is also one of unremitting and unwarranted love. In Luke 11:11, Jesus makes it clear that God as a father loves and provides for his children. In John 15:9, Jesus suggests that his own love for his disciples is a response to the fatherly love of God. John makes it perfectly clear that love is provoked by love, and that *our* love is provoked by *God's* love (1 John 4:19). We need to love our children, in other words, in order to elicit love *from* them. And since unconditional love is what life is all about, we need to give children this love in order to give them a chance in life.

This image is further enhanced in the parable of the prodigal son (Luke 15). The father gives his son freedom to make his own decisions, even if they're foolish. But when his son screws up, rather than saying 'I told you so', the father's heart is broken. He spends his days looking for his son on the horizon, longing for his return. And when he does return, humbled and destitute, the father welcomes him so unreservedly that his other son accuses him of favouritism, a charge the father ardently denies. There is quite enough love in his heart for two very different children.

> **'Children aren't happy with nothing to ignore,
> and that's what parents were created for.'**
>
> American poet Ogden Nash

In the Bible, children were instructed to respect their parents (e.g. Exod. 20:12; Prov. 1:8; 4:1; 6:20; 13:1; 15:5). The way in which this respect should be understood is explained by Paul in Ephesians (6:1–4) and Colossians (3:20, 21): children should obey their parents, but parents should be careful not to embitter or maltreat their children. Exodus 20:12 is not a blanket endorsement of anything a parent might feel like doing. The restraints on parents are as great as the restraints on children.

Hebrews 12:9–10, for instance, tells us that God disciplines his children for their own good. People should benefit from the discipline their parents give them, helping them to learn right from wrong, just as they benefit from the discipline God gives them. Power and responsibility therefore go together. The power to discipline is given only because of parents' responsibility to bring up their children properly.

PARENTING

- God seeks to enjoy a parent/child relationship with each of us, and this is mirrored in the imagery of the Christian faith. God is the ultimate Mother and Father.
- Since we are all children of God, we are *always* somebody's child, even if our own parents are dead.
- As members of the family of the Church, both local and worldwide, we are part of a web of relationships which extends well beyond the narrow confines of the 'nuclear family'.

Engage

Families form the essential backbone of most churches, and parents form the backbone of the family. So parenting is in fact of vital interest to the Church. Here are some ways in which churches can help parents – both the parents in their congregation and those in the surrounding community.

Practical teaching

There are sermons galore on the fatherhood of God, but it's rare to hear one aimed at parenting on a practical level. Good, down-to-earth, commonsense, applied Christian teaching on what it means to be a parent, how to be a parent, and how to survive a parent, could prove very useful for your church. All too often it seems as though Christians are good at talking about God's love, but very poor at showing it or applying it. Useful, practical sermons, based on Christian principles, are every bit as much 'preaching the gospel' as more traditional approaches.

House groups

Your church could run a series of house groups on the issue of parenting, covering everything from conception (for those who want to be parents) to crown court (for those who wish they weren't)! House groups allow you to move away from an atmosphere of 'the expert says' and into more free and open discussion, in which people's *specific* parenting worries can be talked through, and in which encouragement can be given in a personal way.

Child and Parent Centres

The National Society for the Prevention of Cruelty to Children (NSPCC) runs several Child and Parent Centres, open to parents or carers of children up to age 12, free of charge. The Centres offer specialist advice for parents and children alike on a range of different subjects (such as health, children's worries, and self-assertiveness). They also offer parents and children the chance to play together with the help and input of trained childcare professionals. Toy libraries and community information and advice centres provide extra resources. A similar venture on a smaller scale could be attempted by your church, in collaboration with other local churches or the statutory authorities.

Childcare facilities

Why not set up a crèche, mothers and toddlers group, babysitting service, playschool or childminding network? You'll have to adapt your premises accordingly, of course. If your area is saturated with playschools, it might be better to become involved in one of these rather than to set up your own. Carers *must* receive professional training and possess the appropriate professional qualifications, and the church should be involved in sponsoring this 'vocational' training. Again, there should be no hidden agenda: you should serve people with this project, not try to convert them.

**'Men haven't kept up with the changes in society,
they don't know how to be parents.
Nobody has taught them; where are the cultural
institutions to tell them that
being an active parent is a good thing?
They don't exist.
At the same time, women don't have
many expectations of what men might provide.'**

Anna Coote, Institute for Public Policy Research,
The Times, 22nd September 1991

Parenting seminars

Seminars allow for an informal atmosphere in which people can discuss their common problems. They can be structured to include audience participation, and can be more attractive for outsiders than sermons because they are not within the context of a worship service. Arrange seminars for the evening or for breakfast time, so that working parents are not ruled out. You could invite a range of speakers, Christian or not, to talk on various aspects of parenting. For instance, in 1995 Rob Parsons ran a massive seminar tour entitled, 'Loving against the Odds: Issues Families Face'. Care for the Family, of which Rob is director, can offer a range of excellent resources for such seminars.

Holidays

Care for the Family also run special low-cost, Outward Bound-type holidays for single-parent families, offering 'physical and spiritual refreshment', as well as the chance to build a closer relationship between parents and children. There is an equivalent for specific members of two-parent families, in a variety of permutations (father/son, mother/son, father/daughter, mother/daughter). The idea is to allow parent and child to grow closer by doing fun things together and sharing an adventure.

> **'When I was a boy of fourteen,
> my father was so ignorant I could hardly stand to
> have the old man around.
> But when I got to be twenty-one, I was astonished
> at how much he had learned in seven years.'**
>
> Mark Twain

Godparents

In Anglican and Catholic churches, when an infant is baptised, godparents are appointed to help and support the parents in raising the children to become strong, committed Christians. When this task is entered into thoughtfully, it provides a positive support and resource for a child's natural parents. Even if we don't actually want to *baptise* infants, we should encourage the adoption of some kind of Godparent Scheme, in which experienced parents undertake to help out new parents, both with practical help and advice.

> **'The American family is experiencing
> an unprecedented period of disintegration
> which threatens the entire superstructure of our
> society, and we simply must take whatever steps
> are necessary to insure its integrity'**
>
> American paediatrician James Dobson

Sunday tolerance

How many times have you heard people in church complain about the behaviour and noise levels of the young children? Too often we do everything but 'suffer the little children to come unto' Jesus. In fact, when it comes to Sunday mornings, we'd rather not suffer the little children at all! 'After all,' we argue, 'they have Sunday School.' There is a distinct need in a great many churches to educate the church itself about tolerating children: they should actively be *welcomed*, embraced with open arms, and we need to restructure our services in many cases to accommodate this.

Further information

Agencies

Care for the Family, 53 Romney Street, London SW1P 3RF. Tel: 0171-233 0983.

Portsmouth Area Family Concern, 30 Hillside Avenue, Widley, Waterlooville, PO7 5BB.

Christian Child Care Network, 10 Crescent Road, South Woodford, London E18 1JB.

Christian Link Association of Single Parents (CLASP), 'Linden', Shorter Avenue, Shenfield, Essex CM15 8RE.

NSPCC, National Centre, 42 Curtain Road, London EC2A 3NH. Tel: 0171-825 2500.

Publications

Parentwise, 37 Elm Road, New Malden, Surrey KT3 3HB. Tel: 0181-942 9761.

Elizabeth Hartley-Brewer, *Positive Parenting: Raising Children with Self Esteem* (Cedar (Mandarin), 1994). (Not specifically Christian.)

Libby Purves, *How Not To Be a Perfect Family* (HarperCollins, 1994). (Not specifically Christian.)

Help! I'm a Parent. A multi-format resource produced by the Church Pastoral Aid Society, 1994, especially good for use in church and home groups.

Chapter 5

Debt

BARRY IS AN ENGINEER in his late 40s, with a house, a wife, three children, two cats and a dog. He has been in steady employment for over twenty years, when suddenly the bottom drops out of the aeronautic industry, and he is laid off along with hundreds of others. Although he has both experience and qualifications, his age makes it very difficult for him to find another job. He finds himself competing with people who are younger and faster than him, and who are prepared to work for less money. His wife has never had to work, and the redundancy payment isn't enough to pay off his mortgage, let alone the school fees. After nine months of unemployment, Barry is anxious, depressed, confused and demotivated. The constant rows with his wife are becoming increasingly bitter, and she doesn't think she can take much more. The children's school work is suffering, and there are increasing discipline problems with the eldest.

Listen

Debt affects a great many different people and has a devastating impact not just on the person in debt, but also on those around them. But it's not necessarily those who handle money irresponsibly or wastefully who get into debt.

Of course, there are those whose ambition is greater than their wallet will allow, and whose spending on needless things lands them in serious financial difficulties. Keeping up with the Joneses can have devastating consequences. Added to this, those who get addicted to things like gambling or drugs also risk near-certain debt. In fact, *any* kind of addiction transfers control of your life from you to the object of your addiction. And if, as with most addictions, there is a financial price to be paid, this can spiral out of all proportions. Unfortunately, people rarely appreciate the true financial cost of addictions *before* they give them up.

It should be noted, however, that addiction is more frequently the *result* of debt than its cause. How many people take up smoking or heavy drinking because of the stress of their financial worries?

'The incomes of the poorest 10 per cent have fallen by 17 per cent in real terms since the Conservatives came to power, and the number of people living on an income below the European "poverty line" – half the average income – has risen from 5 million to 13.9 million, a quarter of the population in 1991–92.'

Rosie Waterhouse, The Independent, 15th July 1994

The majority of people in debt are there *through little or no fault of their own*. The reasons why they end up in debt are many and varied. The following are just some of the most common.

- Many people leave school at 16 or 18 with few qualifications and little prospect of finding a job. Unskilled labour has never been less in demand, and those unemployed who have never had a job find it very hard to live on whatever benefits they're entitled to, even assuming they know what these are.
- Rising employment figures do not seem able to stem the tide of redundancy. The hardest hit, perhaps, are men who are the only breadwinner in their household, have worked all their lives, and have a mortgage and dependants. At 40-something, they are often less attractive to employers than younger, cheaper people. Made redundant, they can suddenly find that their income is dwarfed by their expenditure.
- Many people's income is determined to a large extent by the amount of overtime they can work, or the number of commis-

sions they can bring in. When these dry up, as they did in the last recession, they move from the black to the red.

- Since there is no national minimum wage, many people in menial jobs can find themselves living below the relative poverty line (half the national average income after the subtraction of housing costs), in spite of the fact that they have jobs. Employers may have, or claim to have, no choice but to pay their workers a substandard wage if they are to continue to stay in business.

- Borrowing too much is a common reason for debt. Often a person overestimates their income or underestimates their expenditure, arranging a loan or buying things on credit when they can't actually afford the repayments.

- Debt can be caused by simple mismanagement of finances. Proper accounting and budgeting skills are rarely taught at school or elsewhere. Without savings and careful budgeting, it's all too easy to be caught out by a rise in mortgage rates, for example, or an increase in bills or council tax.

- Christmas can be a major expense and cause of debt. Low-income families spend almost as much at Christmas time as middle and high income families. In fact, seen as a proportion of their income, they spend a great deal more. The average family spends about £2,000 on Christmas, and many families are prepared to go into debt to pay for it.

- Students are increasingly expected to pay for their own education. Loans come into force at a point when graduates find themselves hard pressed to find a suitable job, lumbering many of the least well-off with crushing debts at the start of their working lives.

- Illness is a frequent cause of debt. If a person is ill beyond the scope of any permitted sick leave, or needs to take time off work to care for a sick relative, they can find themselves descending rapidly into debt.

- The death of a wage-earning partner, the failure of a marriage, or the break-up of a live-in relationship can result in major debts as estates are wound up or assets and incomes divided.

'Look at me: I worked my way up from nothing to a state of extreme poverty.'

Groucho Marx

Once a person is in debt, it can prove almost impossible for them to get out. Poverty, debt and interest repayment are a vicious circle. People find themselves unable to get on top of things until they've paid off their debts, and unable to pay off their debts until they've got on top of things.

Although the causes of debt are many and varied, people's emotional responses to it are more or less uniform: *denial* that the situation is as bad as it is; *fear* of impending doom, specifically of the unknown and uncontrollable; *guilt* about having got into debt in the first place, and about being unable to provide for any dependants; and feelings of *loneliness and isolation*, of being the only person ever to have suffered in quite this way, of being a burden or an outcast. People in debt can feel any or all of these, one at a time or all together. Reactions are often far from rational. To escape from feelings of entrapment, people in debt will frequently refuse to open letters they know to be bills, might eat more, or might even go on spending sprees.

'Poverty does not produce unhappiness; it produces degradation.'

George Bernard Shaw

The effects and implications of debt on a person are as variable as the causes. People are affected in different ways, depending on their circumstances and the ways in which they choose to cope with their plight.

Relate report that in 70 per cent of cases of marriage breakdown, money problems are cited as *the* major factor. Recent research undertaken by Barnardo's (*Unfair Shares*, 1994) claims that the widening gap between rich and poor is having devastating effects. The report concludes that it is *relative*, not *absolute*, poverty which causes distress, depression and the frequent onset of health problems. In other words, it's not how little you have that matters, but how little you have in relation to other people.

Since being in debt implies personal failure, whether or not this is in fact the case, it is almost always accompanied by a profound loss of self-confidence and self-esteem. Ironically, this adds to the problems of a person in debt, since self-confidence is usually a vital factor in recovering from insolvency.

The depression which debt brings in its wake can push relationships to the limit. But this is not merely a pruning of 'fair weather friends' – even *genuine* friendships can suffer.

People who can't repay their credit card bills can find themselves blacklisted as the result of a civil court action. This can push them into the path of loan sharks, whose exorbitant interest demands will just compound the initial debt.

As the ultimate effect, a great many suicide attempts have financial worries at their root, as people find themselves unable to see a way out of their present difficulties, and feel themselves utterly unable to cope.

According to Credit Action:

- Total unpaid debt in Britain (excluding mortgages) has trebled since 1981 to £54 billion (equivalent to £2,400 per household).
- An estimated 4 million households had at least one debt problem in 1993.
- Over 4 million court summonses were issued for debt in 1993.
- About 1.2 million houses are now worth less than their mortgage (negative equity).
- There are about 39 million credit cards in the UK. People with credit cards spend an estimated 34 per cent more than those without.
- Watchdog agencies estimate that 1.5 million households are struggling to pay their electricity bill and 1 million are struggling to pay their gas bill. Disconnections per annum stand at around 70,000 for electricity and 20,000 for gas.
- Approximately one in six people needs income support.
- About half of all single parents are in debt.
- The average total amount of debt per debtor is over £10,000.

According to the Child Poverty Action Group:

- The Income Support Allowance for an 11-year-old child (£15.65 per week, or £2.22 per day) is roughly a quarter of that needed for what they define as a 'modest but adequate' budget (about £56 per week).
- Child Benefit meets only about 35 per cent of the weekly cost of a child in a two–child family. Income support meets only 59 per cent.

Reflect

In order to build a proper understanding of the way in which the Bible views debt, it is first necessary to examine what it has to say on some of the wider issues relating to wealth and the use of resources.

It was against the law, for instance, for the Israelites to charge each other interest on loans. God commands in Exodus 22:25: 'If you lend money to one of my people amongst you, don't be like a money-lender: charge them no interest. If you take a neighbour's coat as a pledge [collateral], return it to them by sunset, since it's the only covering they have.' To lend money *for interest* was considered a selfish act, one which was against the community. It was beneath an Israelite to lend money for interest to another Israelite. (See also: Leviticus 25:35–37; Deuteronomy 23:19; Psalm 15:5; Proverbs 19:17 and 28:8.)

It was, however, considered acceptable for an Israelite to lend money to a foreigner for interest (Deut. 23:20), or to lend money to a fellow Israelite for collateral (but see the restrictions placed upon this in Deuteronomy 24:10–13, and the condemnations for ignoring these restrictions in Job 24:3, 9).

The point of these strong laws is the idea of Israel as a community, as a people. The people of Israel were meant to carry one another through their times of trouble, not seize the opportunity to profit from another's misfortune. This same sense of community can be seen in the early Church (Acts 4:32–37), and in Jesus' extension of the family beyond mere blood relatives (Matt. 12:46–50).

It was therefore permissible to lend money to fellow Israelites, but the idea behind this was to help them, not to help yourself by them! If money was borrowed, the statute of limitations on the debt was generally seven years (Deut. 15). Every forty-nine years, debts were to be cancelled totally, and all property outside a city wall was returned to its original owners.

This year of debt cancellation was known as the Jubilee, and the principle behind it was simple: 'The land must not be sold permanently, because the land is mine and you are but aliens and my tenants' (Lev. 25:23). We are only stewards and should act accordingly. This idea had been implicit in the nomadic existence of the people of Israel before Joseph, and in their status as immigrants in Egypt before Moses. But with the Promised Land fast becoming reality, it was necessary for the principle to be enshrined in law. (It was re-emphasised after the Babylonian exile, in Nehemiah 10:31.)

It's highly likely that the Jubilee law was never practised properly. Ruth 2 suggests that the provisions for widows and aliens (Deut. 24:17–22) were followed at least occasionally, and Ruth 4 records that Boaz redeemed the debt according to the provisions of the law. But the frequency with which the prophets railed against the Israelites for their fraudulent treatment of the land and neglect of the poor and defenceless makes it clear that even if the letter of the law was followed, the spirit was roundly ignored.

Isaiah contrasted the theft of the poor's possessions (3:14) and the denial of justice to them (10:2) by Israel with the strong defence of the poor by God (25:4). Jeremiah (22:16) compared the behaviour of the good king Josiah, who 'defended the cause of the poor and needy', with that of his son, Shallum, who extended his palace and decorated it in cedar 'through unrighteousness'. And Ezekiel (18:8) described the righteous man as 'someone who does not lend at usury or take interest'.

> **'Poverty makes people sub-human.**
> **Excess of wealth makes people inhuman.'**
>
> Retired Brazilian Archbishop Helder Camara

Proverbs 22:16 suggests that generosity is its own reward (cf. verse 9), and that bribery and exploitation are their own ruin. Jesus himself picks up on this with the parable of the shrewd manager (Luke 16). This foreman had no defence for his corrupt waste of his master's estate, but knew enough to make friends using his master's money before leaving his employ. Whilst Jesus doesn't necessarily approve of the manager's behaviour, he advises his followers to use their money to make friends rather than profit. 'No slave can serve two masters,' he argues; 'they will hate one and love the other, or will endure one and despise the other. You cannot serve both God and money' (cf. Matt. 6:24; 1 Tim. 6:6–10).

The same idea occurs in the parable of the rich fool (Luke 12:13–21). In the story, God calls the rich man 'stupid' because he builds bigger barns to store precious but perishable grain rather than using this excess to feed the less well off. 'For what use is it for a person to gain the whole world and yet lose their soul?' (Matt. 16:26; Luke 9:25). It is clear that investment should be in *people*, not profit margins.

> **'If we show partiality to the wealthy,**
> **then we are not free, because we are still slaves to**
> **the mentality that says that power and riches are**
> **more important than love.**
> **If we do this, we do not have God's Spirit**
> **controlling our lives.'**
>
> Nicaraguan doctor Gustavo Parajon

You might be wondering what this has to do with those in debt; after all, it has more to do with lenders than with borrowers. The reason for this is that the Bible *is* more concerned with lenders than with borrowers, anxious that those at a disadvantage should not be further exploited. The aim of lending money should be to help those in need to stand on their own two feet again.

Quite clearly, 'the rich rule over the poor, and the borrower is servant to the lender' (Prov. 22:7). Today, money is lent not to improve the lot of the community, but to increase the bank balance of the lender. It's no mere coincidence that the literal derivation of the word 'mortgage' is 'death pledge'.

What we can learn from this, however, is that Old Testament law was structured to *minimise* short-term debt, and to *eliminate* long-term debt. Our approach to those who are in debt must therefore be to help them to get out of debt. After all, the 'good news to the poor' of Isaiah 61 and Luke 4 *cannot* be that they will continue to be poor. This would hardly be good news.

DEBT

- In the Old Testament, debt was considered misfortune for the person in debt, for their family, and for their community at large. The onus was on the community to help the debtor out of their debt.
- Taking advantage of a person's poverty or debt was considered a major sin both by the law and by the prophets.
- Jesus' approach to debt was to forgive what couldn't be repaid, in the same way that you would like to have your own unrepayable debts cancelled (see Matthew 6:12 and 18:21–25).

Engage

Debt is a very common problem, but, strange as it may seem, not one that can be solved simply by throwing money at it. Here are four ways, however, in which you and your church can help.

1. *Education* about debt and its consequences for both children and adults, those in debt and those not, is a vital first step. All too often, debt is something nobody talks about. Pride is part of human nature, and debt is considered shameful. This can be especially so for Christians who find themselves in debt, and have to reconcile their situation with the Church's teaching on stewardship, and therefore wrestle with feelings of guilt. You can be pretty sure that there are committed Christians in your church who are struggling with debt.

Raising awareness of the issue must be done sensitively through practical, down-to-earth teaching, explaining how people get into and out of debt. Specialist groups such as Credit Action can help with this, providing materials and speakers with considerable experience in this area.

2. *Pastoral counselling*. The stress of being in debt can exacerbate otherwise minor niggles and project them to epic proportions. The consequences of debt go far beyond the immediate impact of lacking money. It is important for a church to be prepared to give pastoral support to those whose lives and families are suffering as a result of going into debt.

Setting up a debt counselling service can help enormously. This is a perfect opportunity for members of the church to get involved, although it's very important that, as with everything a local church does to reach out into the community, it should be run properly. As people are encouraged to talk about their worries and their fears, counsellors will find themselves on the receiving end of some strong emotions. It's therefore vital that you screen candidates carefully, and provide them with proper pastoral training and support.

It is probable, unless your church is very big, that you will find yourself stretched to come up with enough qualified personnel to run an effective service. Do not fear. Since debt is not a limited or denominational issue, it makes sense that your solution should not confine itself to one church or denomination. This could provide you with an excellent project either to start or to continue a working relationship with other churches in your area.

3. *Financial counselling*. A debt counselling service is not just about providing a shoulder to cry on: it's also about money management. People in debt want help to get out of it, and this help should be a mixture of moral support and financial advice. If you are going to dole out financial advice, be sure that it is both sensible and sound. Bad advice could land people in worse trouble than they started with.

Because of this, financial advice, other than in the broadest terms, is governed by the Financial Services Act. (For more information, contact Credit Action.)

People in debt will need first to come to terms with their own situation; facing up to this can often require great courage. It also requires them sharing with their partner, if they have one, and the financial aspects of counselling may well be best conducted with the couple together. They will need help in how to approach their creditors, who can sometimes be sympathetic if they are aware of the problems and can be assured that they will be repaid in time. Credit Action estimate that about 20 per cent of people who seek financial advice from them are not receiving benefits for which they are eligible. A considerable amount of help can be given simply by offering advice on how to budget properly.

> **'Britain is a wealthy country.**
> **There is no excuse for this level of poverty**
> **and we should be deeply ashamed.'**
>
> Sally Witcher, Child Poverty Action Group

4. *Practical help.* It is very important, when considering practical help, to choose ways of helping that will restore dignity and self-respect. For instance, mothers' groups can be a good way of channelling help such as passed-on children's clothing, baby-sitting, shared meals, lifts to the shops, or to the Department of Social Services, or to church. Church notice sheets can be used to advertise extra work such as gardening or DIY for those on a low income or in part-time work.

On a larger and more ambitious scale, there is no reason why your church could not join with other churches in the area to offer some form of local credit union. Credit unions are non-profit-making bodies, run by volunteers, providing a savings and loan service for their 'members'. Anyone can be a member, provided they agree to keep the rules, and have something in common with other members. When you join a credit union, all your outstanding debts are usually 'consolidated': i.e., paid off at once by the union. You then repay this at minimal interest over an agreed period of time. Members are encouraged to deposit money as savings, and are usually allowed to borrow twice as much as they invest. Credit unions can help people learn how to save and budget, as well as enabling them to enjoy things that they would never otherwise be able to afford, such as holidays.

Further information

Agencies

Credit Action, Jubilee Centre, 3 Hooper Street, Cambridge, CB1 2NZ. Tel: 01223 324034, for speakers and materials.

Church Action on Poverty, Central Buildings, Oldham Street, Manchester M1 1JT. Tel: 0161-236 9321, campaigning for change.

Association of British Credit Unions, Unit 307, Westminster Business Square, 33 Kennington Lane, London SE11 5QY, for advice on setting up a credit union.

Books

Keith Tondeur, *Escape from Debt* and *Helping People In Debt*, both available from Credit Action.

Chapter 6

The National Lottery

'BUGBOX' IN HAND, each of my children has, in turn, made the discovery that under every one of the hundreds of stones in our back garden lurks a multitude of creepy-crawlies. In many ways, the National Lottery is just like one of those stones. What seems at first to be one simple issue – and, at the cost of a pound a shot, many would argue a reasonably harmless one – turns out on closer inspection to be camouflaging a host of complex moral issues which we cannot afford to ignore.

Listen

Tickets for the National Lottery went on sale on 14th November 1994. Camelot, the company which won the franchise over seven other applicants, is licensed by the government under the provisions of the National Lottery Act, 1993, to run the Lottery until the year 2001. The last time there was a national lottery in Britain was in 1826.

Camelot is a consortium of five companies: Cadbury Schweppes, the drinks manufacturer; ICL, which makes computers and software; De La Rue, which prints banknotes and instant lottery tickets for different countries; Racal, the electronic communications company; and the American GTECH Corporation, the world's leading manufacturer of lottery hardware. Together their capital investment in the Lottery was roughly £125 million, but they have already made a huge profit.

Initial rivalry between the Lottery organisers and the established bookmakers and gambling merchants, including the various football pools companies, suggested that the majority of Lottery entrants would be switching their allegiance. Camelot moved to calm these fears by suggesting that they would not so much poach from the pools as attract new customers, or even entice pools players to enter the Lottery as well. In other words, by their own admission, their goal has been and is to increase the number of people 'having a go', and to increase the amount spent by those who already gamble. It's reckoned that 80 per cent of the adult population are within easy reach of a shop selling Lottery tickets. Camelot's budget for advertising and promotion for the first year alone was £40 million. Commercial Operations Director, Norman Hawkins, said that the aim was simply to 'encourage people to have a flutter'.

'I did not think the government should encourage more gambling.'

Former Prime Minister Margaret Thatcher, explaining why she had rejected the Lottery idea

The first week of the Lottery, which failed to produce the expected millionaire, resulted in an unexpected 1,152,611 winners competing for a total payout of £22,004,123. Since the payout is half the revenue gathered from ticket sales, this means that 44,008,246 entries were made by an estimated 25 million people, roughly 55 per cent of the UK over-16 population. (Market research indicates that roughly 75 per cent of British adults gamble in one way or another every year.) But when the jackpot rolled over for the second week running, in January 1996 – to a total of £42 million – Camelot estimated that almost 90 per cent of the eligible population had bought a ticket.

The odds of winning the jackpot are almost fourteen million to one – an extremely long shot in anyone's book. Playing £1 a week every week, it could take you as long as 270,000 years to win! But if the odds of winning a £10 prize seem more appealing, remember that with odds of 57:1 you would have to spend, on average, £57 to win £10, a shortfall of £47!

Instant-win scratchcards were introduced in March 1995, a separate game from the National Lottery but also organised by

Camelot, aimed at exploiting the Lottery tie-in. With this, people know immediately whether or not they've won a prize of up to £50,000. 'Instants', as they're known, cause perhaps the greatest concern, as some people just can't resist the temptation to keep buying cards until they win or run out of money, even if it means that they win less in the end than they spend on cards in the first place.

When the government first seriously debated setting up a National Lottery, they suggested that it would be a good means of raising extra capital for both cultural organisations and charities. Some of the initial advertising, and spokespeople for both Camelot and the government, played up the Lottery's donations to 'good causes'. But most of the advertising for the Lottery has been more honest, appealing to greed rather than compassion: '*It could be YOU!*'

But does it help charities? In fact, an average of just 5.6 per cent of the gross proceeds of the Lottery goes to charity. Camelot claimed that once the Lottery was running at peak, it would produce around £308 million per annum (£5.9 million per week) for charities from an estimated total annual gross income of £5.5 billion (£105 million per week). By contrast, about £2.7 billion (50 per cent) goes out in prize money, a total weekly payout of around £52 million.

Most of the major charities have come out against the Lottery, many citing the precedent in Ireland, where about 4 per cent of those who bought tickets for the state lottery, introduced in 1987, said that they would otherwise have given the money to charity. Provisional figures, produced after the first year by the National Council for Voluntary Organisations (NCVO), suggest that the trend in the UK is higher, and that almost 6.5 per cent of the money spent on Lottery tickets would otherwise have gone to charities.

The NCVO estimates that UK charities lost income worth a total of £339 million in the Lottery's first year. Since, according to NCVO estimates, the first year's payout to charities from the Lottery was just £248 million, this means that charities as a whole lost roughly £91 million during 1995 as a result of the National Lottery. If, *at peak*, Camelot raises £308 million a year for charity, charities can still expect an eventual net *loss* of £31 million – more if increased lottery fever makes direct giving drop even further.

To obtain a grant, charities need to submit an application for funds to the National Lottery Charities Board, an independent body appointed by the Home Office and charged with distributing money raised by the Lottery and allocated to 'charities'. Each application is assessed on its merits, but with a limited pot and huge demand, charities must compete with each other to show that they would make the most effective use of the money.

Some larger charities have traditionally relied on lottery-type fundraising, and are hoping that Lottery fever will actually improve their income. Many of the big, well-established charities, however, reckon that they will be largely unaffected, since the majority of their income is from regular giving by committed donors. But they still see the Lottery as unhealthy and potentially damaging for smaller charities, which find it hardest to raise money. Those small charities unsuccessful in bidding for Lottery money can only expect to lose out.

In addition to this, it's reasonable, on the basis of government policy toward public expenditure, to expect that 'good causes' in the world of arts, sports and heritage will experience a freeze or a drop in government subsidy. Although Lottery money can only be given to 'new projects', and is forbidden to replace existing funding, it has to be asked if the government wouldn't have ended up funding some of these new projects itself if it weren't for the Lottery.

Lottery money also goes to the Millennium Fund, a special fund organised to 'celebrate the Millennium'. No one – including, it seems, the Millennium Commission set up to distribute the money – appears to be entirely clear about what this means. Simon Jenkins, a member of the Millennium Commission, told *The Daily Telegraph* (1st May 1995) that most applications had exploited the confusion by 'simply calling whatever it is they want millennial'. They had received applications for millennium towers, bridges, museums, universities, medical centres, forests, footpaths, cliffs, stadiums, church halls, and community centres. One group had even applied for £1 million just to think about the millennium! In fact, the situation was so confused that in January 1996, Prince Charles controversially involved himself by suggesting that the celebration of the millennium was in danger of becoming one 'giant meaningless party', with the fund being spent on worthless ideas rather than being used to enhance the social and spiritual life of the country.

Although all Lottery prizes are tax free, the Inland Revenue takes 12 per cent of the overall income. If, over time, this hits Camelot's annual target of £5.5 billion, the government will receive an extra £660 million tax per annum thanks to the Lottery. According to figures provided by David Smith, Economics Editor of *The Sunday Times*, this is the equivalent of putting an extra 0.3 pence on the basic rate of income tax.

> **'Every man and woman in this country can be a direct beneficiary.'**
>
> Prime Minister John Major in The Sunday Times,
> 13th November 1994

Although the winners of big prizes are offered counselling and legal and financial advice, concern has been raised from a number of quarters that instant windfalls can create more problems than they solve. An improvement in lifestyle can decrease misery, but it rarely brings happiness. Many people remember 1960s pools winner Vivienne Nicholson, who announced to the world at large, 'I'm going to spend, spend, spend!' Winners rarely have experience in handling large sums of money, and even with the best advice can find that it evaporates faster than they realise. In addition, studies from America suggest that sudden massive lottery winnings can create guilt in the winner, and jealousy mixed with unreasonable demands and expectations in their friends and relations, who are sure to find out in spite of the promised guarantee of anonymity.

The whole town of Mhasla, India, for instance, celebrated the good fortune of its famous £17.8 million jackpot-winning son – the first really big winner from the Lottery. It didn't seem to matter that he and his entire family lived in Blackburn, England, or that, according to Islamic law, the money was tainted. *The Times of India* reported that a 'fast friend' of the family telephoned London when he heard of the win: 'I congratulated [the winner's brother-in-law] and told him not to forget his old friends.' It's hardly surprising that the winner's father-in-law warned, 'They shouldn't come back to India. In England they will be safe.'

The social displacement this kind of big win can bring in its wake has caused the most concern. Many critics, convinced that the Lottery is here to stay, like it or not, have suggested a number of reforms which they claim will 'improve' the game by lessening the amount of social displacement produced. Amongst the most talked-about measures are capping the jackpot to a level which wouldn't alienate winners from the community – figures anywhere from £100,000 to £1 million have been mentioned – or, alternatively, staggering the payments, as some American states do, so that winners receive their prize over the course of many years.

'Our chief concern is that it is a tax on the poor for the benefit of the comfortably-off. When did you last see a poor person going to the Royal Opera House? This is morally reprehensible and we are deeply unhappy about it.'

Geraldine Ranson of the Methodist Church, in The Sunday Times, 13th November 1994

The most pernicious aspect of the National Lottery, however, must surely be its appeal to lower-income families, many of whom can ill afford even the price of a ticket, at least not on a regular basis. Although £1 may not seem much, most people spend more. I recently met a woman whose financial situation was so desperate that she hadn't eaten for five days. Instead, she'd spent the little money she had on Lottery Instants in the hopes of 'winning my way out of my misery'. Along with a great many others, she shared the feelings of the unemployed Glaswegian woman who told reporters how she borrowed money to buy Instants scratchcards:

'I don't want to buy them, but I cannot help it. The tickets are a possible route out of here' *(Today,* 17th April 1995). But with the odds of winning £50,000 on a scratchcard set at 2.4 million to one, the hope they represent to people on a low income is clearly false. A more accurate slogan for the Lottery might be: *'It won't be YOU!'*

Each player's average expenditure on the Lottery, not including scratchcards, is between £2 and £3 per week. Camelot and the government deny that the poor and those on income-related benefits are likely to buy more Lottery tickets than others. However, this argument misses the point: £3 per week amounts to a significantly higher expenditure as a proportion of some people's total earnings than it does for others.

But added to this, there is evidence to suggest that lower-income families *do* spend more than £2–£3 per week. One north London shopkeeper told *The Independent* (12th April 1995): 'On average, most of my customers spend between £3 and £5 a time. Very few just spend a quid. A lot of them are pensioners, and you feel they are spending money they can't afford. £1 is all right, but £5 means they must be going without something else.'

Dr Sue Fisher, secretary of the European Association for the Study of Gambling, cited an American study *(The Independent,* 11th November 1994) showing that the big spenders in state lotteries tend to come from inner cities, ethnic minorities and low-income groups. Though it's impossible to tell in the short term whether the American trend will bear out here, almost one-quarter of the total UK population receives some form of income-related benefit, and prime-time TV coverage – together with expensive advertising that plays up the potential winnings whilst playing down the probable odds – are perhaps most seductive to those with the greatest need for money.

Critics have argued that the National Lottery franchise gave Camelot a 'licence to print money', and that future operators will not enjoy they same level of profit. Although the Lottery is here to stay, they suggest that pressure coming from various sources will convince future governments to curb its excesses. Since big jackpots, which are likely to be the first target of reforms, are instrumental in enticing people to play, this could hit operators hard.

What's more, Camelot's own success, which has exceeded its expectations, may count against franchise operators in the long run, prompting the government to reduce their percentage take.

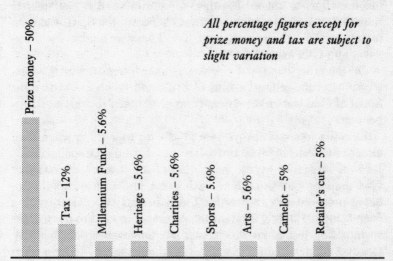

All percentage figures except for prize money and tax are subject to slight variation

Prize money – 50%
Tax – 12%
Millennium Fund – 5.6%
Heritage – 5.6%
Charities – 5.6%
Sports – 5.6%
Arts – 5.6%
Camelot – 5%
Retailer's cut – 5%

The odds of winning a prize are estimated by Camelot as follows: Jackpot: matching six main numbers: 1 in 13,983,816; matching five main numbers plus the bonus number: 1 in 2,330,636; matching five main numbers: 1 in 55,492; matching four main numbers: 1 in 1,033; matching three main numbers: 1 in 57.

Reflect

Gambling is not a big issue in the Bible. And, of course, there was no great Israelite State Lottery. The only time a disembodied hand was seen in biblical times was not in giant, glowing proportions in Lottery advertising, but in the episode of the writing on the wall, when God passed judgment on the ill-fated Belshazzar (Daniel 5).

Drawing lots, however, does exist in the Bible. This was done using pebbles, very much like the National Lottery, and for a variety of reasons. It was, in and of itself, neutral, and the Bible contains examples of both good and bad use.

For instance, drawing lots was used *positively* as a method for choosing the division of land and duties in Leviticus 16:8; Joshua 18:8–10; 1 Chronicles 24–26; Nehemiah 10:34 and 11:1; and, perhaps most famously, in Acts 1:26, when the remaining eleven apostles drew lots to choose Matthias as apostle number twelve after the death of Judas Iscariot. On these occasions, the Spirit was seen to operate through the drawing of lots. Today we tend to use interviews and CVs instead!

On the other hand, drawing lots is linked *negatively* with idolatry and fortune-telling in Ezekiel 21:21 and Jonah 1:7, where the Spirit of God was either absent from or opposed to what was happening.

Drawing lots was always viewed as a *negative* thing when used either as a means of social provision or in dividing the spoils of war. Job was staggered by the accusation of his 'friend' Eliphaz that God must be punishing him for his sins, and accused Eliphaz of being prepared to cast lots for the fatherless and barter away a friend (Job 6:27). Joel brought the judgment of God to the nations surrounding Jerusalem which 'cast lots for my people' (Joel 3:3). Obadiah condemned the Edomites for doing nothing to help when the Babylonians 'cast lots for Jerusalem' (Obadiah verse 11). Nahum warned Nineveh, the capital of the mighty Assyrian Empire, that they were in danger of going the way of the Egyptian city, Thebes, which was destroyed and obliterated, with lots cast for the city's VIPs (Nahum 3:10).

It may come as a surprise to find that gambling does not feature prominently in the Bible. People from nonconformist backgrounds are conditioned to think of gambling as being roundly condemned on every page! But the truth is that the Bible takes a pretty much neutral line on the subject. There are strong similarities here with the drink issue. The Church's response to alcohol – which the Bible doesn't condemn – has frequently been muddled and confused, with a great many people trying to invent a biblical position that simply doesn't exist, all in the interests of clarity and responsibility.

For instance, Paul did *not* instruct Timothy to use wine as an alcohol rub; he told him to *drink* it, because unpurified water was probably giving him amoebic dysentery (1 Tim. 5:23). Similarly, the guests at the wedding in Cana weren't so drunk or incompetent that they mistook non-alcoholic grape juice for vintage wine (John 2:9–10). Jesus himself was accused of being 'a glutton and a drunkard' (Matt. 11:19). Drunkenness is a problem known in the Bible from Noah onwards, but Jesus and Paul, like the Old Testament writers, still managed to steer a responsible line about the right use of alcohol without preaching teetotalism.

If the Bible is neutral about lotteries *per se*, however, as it's neutral about alcohol *per se*, it is definitely *not* ambivalent about the issues surrounding them. Arguments against the National Lottery come down to four major issues: the seduction of the poor, the encouragement of greed, hypocrisy, and the encouragement of addiction.

1. *Poverty*. Jeremiah had nothing against cedar panelling itself. What outraged him about King Shallum's interior redecoration plans (Jer. 22:11–17) was that they were carried out at the expense of the poor. Shallum, the son of the great King Josiah, built his palace with 'unrighteousness' and 'injustice', whilst his father 'defended the cause of the poor and the needy'. The Old Testament is clearly stacked in favour of the poor. You only have to look up words such as 'poor', 'widow', 'alien' or 'fatherless' in a concordance to discover just how central this concern is.

In the New Testament, Jesus suggests that his prophetic mission is to preach good news to the poor (which can't be that they will continue to be poor; Luke 4:18), and that his followers are to treat society's 'insignificants' as though they were Christ himself (Matt. 25:40). The kingdom of God belongs to the poor, he argues (Matt. 5:3; Luke 6:20).

The Church simply cannot endorse a National Lottery which takes from the poor (albeit by seduction rather than theft) and gives back to the better-off (in the form of artificially reduced income tax), like some inverted Robin Hood.

'We are supposed to be working for the poorest people, who have already lost in one lottery – I don't want them to lose in another.'

Michael Taylor, Director of Christian Aid

2. *Greed.* The Bible has a lot to say about greed and selfishness. Essentially, greed is about putting yourself and your own needs and desires ahead of those of other people. It is a reversal of the Christian ethic – 'love your neighbour as yourself' (Lev. 19:18) – because it states, in effect, 'love yourself *at the expense of* your neighbour'.

Lottery critics sometimes cite the often devastating effects on the poor of the eighteenth- and early nineteenth-century versions of a national lottery in Britain, as evidence that people can be sucked into a get-rich-quick philosophy and seduced by greed. If, that is, greed was not their motivation in the first place.

Making allusions to Jeremiah's warnings to Shallum, Jesus told the parable of the rich fool, who spent money to build bigger barns to house the excess of a crop he could never possibly use, rather than giving it to those who could have used it more constructively. 'Stupid! Tonight your life will be taken from you, and then who will get your investment?' Jesus concluded. 'So it is with those who store up treasures for themselves but are not rich toward God' (Luke 12:13–21).

3. *Hypocrisy.* The National Lottery has made a virtue of its charitable donations, even though an average of just 5 pence from each £1 ticket goes to registered charities. Advertising which appeared two weeks before the launch claimed, 'every time you play the National Lottery, someone else gets a better chance. Everyone wins.' Yet the reality is that charities are *losing* money from people deciding to play the Lottery rather than giving directly to them.

By encouraging greed in the name of generosity, the Lottery not only locks into the 'greed is the creed' mentality predominant in the 1980s, it also promotes hypocrisy. And you don't have to wander far into the prophets or the gospels to find out what God thinks about that.

4. *Addiction.* Addiction is the acquired dependence upon something. Since the nature of addiction is that it takes over your life, becoming *the* factor which determines everything else, it is essentially a form of idolatry: giving absolute authority to something unworthy of that authority, something other than God.

It used to be argued that any form of gambling would lead inevitably and inexorably into full gambling addiction. Buying a raffle ticket was the 'thin end of the wedge'. But this is just *not* true. Taking one sip of wine will no more make you an alcoholic than eating one biscuit will make you a glutton. The process isn't automatic.

Nevertheless, there is still a real danger that the National Lottery could hook more people on gambling than are presently 'caught', and could increase the addiction in those who already gamble. Those in lower-income families, who have little chance of escaping their poverty, are especially vulnerable. The Lottery offers them the hope of ending the cause of their problems in one fell swoop. It doesn't matter that this hope is false, or that the chances of winning the jackpot are fourteen million against. The Lottery offers the tiniest ray of hope to people who live without hope. And this 'false' hope can be powerfully addictive, even when it actually begins to increase their poverty.

THE NATIONAL LOTTERY

- The Lottery is seductive. It encourages people who can't afford it to seek a way out of their problems through gambling rather than prudence and responsibility. It sells people an unrealistic dream at the expense of their reality.
- The Lottery is a bad way of giving to charity. It encourages greed as opposed to generosity, and charities are actually losing money because of it.
- The Lottery encourages the exaltation of money above such things as love, beauty, kindness, compassion, peace and work. It turns money into a god, not a tool.

Engage

So if we suspect that the Lottery is immoral, because it takes surreptitiously from the poor and rewards the rich, what should we do about it?

Think

The first thing to do is to think through your position regarding the Lottery, and the issues surrounding it, very carefully. Traditional knee-jerk reactions will not do if we want people both inside and outside the Church, especially the young, to take us seriously. Half-baked ideas can do more damage than silence.

Set out the issues clearly for your church

You can't simply impose your views on others, and there will almost certainly be those in your congregation who still wish to 'have a flutter'. Look beyond the old 'gambling-is-wrong', 'thin-end-of-the-wedge' apologetics of a half-century ago. It's your task to unpack the Bible rather than just pronounce, 'Thus saith the Lord.'

I know of one church which produced a special pastoral guidelines paper, 'Thoughts on the Lottery', and sent it to every church member. You could make the Lottery the subject of a sermon, or discuss it at the youth group, Sunday School, mums' coffee morning, senior citizens' club, home groups, or whatever meetings your church has.

Be careful not to be dogmatic, and avoid making autocratic policy statements. Your task is not to brainwash people, but to help them focus the issues and think them through carefully for themselves.

Avoid being negative

The next step is *not* to explain to people outside your church why you think the Lottery is wrong, although you should be prepared with reasons for your position if you are asked (cf. 1 Peter 3:15). But be very careful how you do this: great sensitivity and tact are required.

In Britain, most people outside the Church consider it to be a bunch of fuddy-duddy reactionaries who serve a God intent on ruining everyone's fun. The Church always seems to come across as the school headmaster, keen on telling people what is wrong with their lives and behaviour, but never what is right. In communicating with people beyond the Church, it is absolutely vital that you present your arguments in *commonsense* ways, and that you avoid being negative. Present more *good news* than bad.

'I do not believe in a government resorting to a national lottery as a disguise for what ought to be properly thought-out policies . . . the lottery is a hugely regrettable step and my serious response and witness is never to buy a ticket.'

Former President of the Methodist Conference, Dr Leslie Griffiths

Address the wider issues

Many people enter the Lottery in order to win money which they feel would improve the quality of their lives. Amongst poorer members of society, this is not window dressing: things are genuinely hopeless. People who see the Lottery as a way of ending their financial problems, for instance, could benefit enormously from being taught effective ways of managing their finances. So your church should consider setting up a financial advice and debt counselling service (see the last chapter). And since debt and financial worries can occur just as easily within the Church as outside it, practical teaching and seminars on handling money and budgeting would also help with the underlying issues. Above all, we must present realistic alternatives to the Lottery. If it seems to be a (false) hope for the hopeless, we must present people with a genuine source of hope.

Need is, of course, not the only motive underlying people's flirtation with the Lottery. Greed is just as common, if not more so. Greed is a major player in our materialistic society, just as it has been throughout history. If we are serious about engaging popular culture, and not merely remaining in our Christian ghetto, then we will have to tackle issues like greed head-on. This may not win us too many friends, but we cannot easily remain silent and continue to call ourselves Christian.

Applied biblical teaching in sermons, seminars, home groups and evangelistic meetings is the simplest way of discussing this. You should also welcome any opportunity to debate the issue in the wider community. The Lottery provides a very effective focus for thinking about greed and its prevalence in society, especially because most people who enter the Lottery do *not* see themselves as being motivated by greed.

In spite of the amount we congratulated ourselves during the 1980s on the depth of the great British pocket, we are not actually very generous as a nation. We have more in common with Scrooge than with Father Christmas. The reason for this is partly an ignorance of how to give to charity, and which charities to favour. There are thousands of charities which do good work, all reliant on public generosity, and a variety of different ways to give, some more effective than others. Oasis Trust, the charity for which I work, has produced a leaflet detailing ten ways to give, and this could quite easily be adapted for teaching people how to give efficiently to any charity.

Alternatively, why not start or adopt a special community project, such as establishing a children's playscheme or purchasing a new piece of vital equipment for the local hospital, encouraging people to give to *that* rather than to the Lottery?

Further information

About the Lottery

Methodist Church Division of Social Responsibility, Westminster Central Hall, 1 Central Buildings, Westminster, London SW1H 9NH. Tel: 0171-222 8010.

About giving to charity

Oasis Trust, 87 Blackfriars Road, London, SE1 8HA. Tel: 0171-928 9422.

About financial advice

Credit Action, Jubilee Centre, 3 Hooper Street, Cambridge, CB1 2NZ. Tel: 01223 324034.

Chapter 7

Racism

SOMEHOW IT'S ALWAYS the extremists: it's never us. It's Derek Beackon, the former BNP councillor for Millwall in the Isle of Dogs. It's 'Combat 18', causing racially-motivated violence at football matches. We've seen images of racists on the TV and read about them in the newspapers: they are ignorant and stupid and they don't have much hair. And the one thing we know about them is this: they are not us.

But is it really that simple?

Listen

Today, Britain contains people whose origins are from almost every country in the world. About three million people currently living in Britain claim to belong to 'black', 'Asian', 'African', 'Chinese' or other communities, half of whom were born and brought up here, many of whom can speak more than one language.

A century ago, the population of black and Asian people was concentrated in cities such as London and Liverpool, but today it isn't possible to make such generalisations. As immigrants and the children of immigrants have prospered and improved their surroundings, moving to the suburbs, racism has become less and less an exclusively 'inner-city' problem. There is as much racism in Sevenoaks as there is in Stepney.

Racism comes in two forms: blatant and insidious. *Blatant* is when you dislike somebody for their colour and admit it quite openly. *Insidious* is when you either don't admit it, or are unaware of it altogether.

When most people think of racism, they think of blatant forms of racism: slavery, colonialism, Adolf Hitler's 'Final Solution', apartheid, segregation, the murder of people like Stephen Lawrence, name-calling, the desecration of Jewish cemeteries, skinhead violence, neo-Nazi rallies, being spat upon or set fire to or denied a job simply because you're not white.

> **'You know, we must always remember that these black women are not like our women. They don't want their children with them. They really enjoy being alone and being away from their families.'**
>
> A former South African Minister for Bantu Affairs

The parents of one of my first girlfriends didn't like me because they considered me a 'half-caste', since my mother is white and my father was Asian. They told me to my face that I wasn't suitable son-in-law material. After all, they pointed out to their daughter, if she married me, what would our children be like? They could be 'throw-backs'. They could turn out 'as black as the ace of spades' and illiterate.

But a lot of racism is unseen by society as a whole. This insidious racism is often subconscious. It can take the form of prejudices that lie dormant for years until something triggers them off, or assumptions and opinions that people genuinely don't think of as being racist.

The first, *dormant* variety is illustrated in the film, *Guess Who's Coming to Dinner*. Spencer Tracy and Katharine Hepburn consider themselves a genial and liberal couple until their daughter brings home Sidney Poitier with marriage plans. Emotional shocks can bring out well-buried racial prejudices, and reveal the kind of attitude toward people of other cultural backgrounds that the ancient Hebrews held toward the prophets: everyone loved a prophet, but not in their own backyard. I remember clearly, for instance, visiting the house of an elderly Christian, a godly man for whom I have great respect. The first million-pound transfer deal for a black football player was announced on television while I was there and my host, in spite of himself, cried out in astonishment, 'A million pounds *for a black man*!'

The second, *active* variety of insidious racism is slightly different. For example, a friend's child, one of a small minority of black children in a Kent school, reported the words of a well-meaning white teacher: 'Some black people are very nice; in fact, some black people are nicer than white people!' It simply didn't occur to the teacher concerned that this statement was racist. Behind active insidious racism is the assumption by white people that white is *normal* – and that black or Asian deviates from this norm – rather than seeing humanity as a rainbow.

'I want to be the white man's brother, not his brother-in-law.'

Martin Luther King, Jr

America during the civil rights era provides an excellent example of both types of racism, both blatant and insidious. Northern white liberals condemned the blatant racism of the South, where schools, buses, restaurants, drinking fountains, toilets, housing and jobs were all segregated, and where black men couldn't look at white men as equals without being shot. Yet many Northern liberals seemed genuinely unaware that schools and housing were also segregated in the North. Not in law, perhaps, but in reality. So when Northern cities like Cleveland and Los Angeles erupted in race riots, white residents were genuinely surprised.

As well as being personal, racism can be *systemic*: that is, it can characterise the behaviour of a system, regardless of the attitudes and actions of the people in that system. Society can have different mechanisms for keeping people 'in their place', without the need for most people to realise that these mechanisms even exist.

American educator Jonathan Kozol explains what this means in terms of the US school system. Looking at a top New York school, which has an open admissions policy but where only 4.6 per cent of students are black, Kozol remarks, 'That's an excellent example of conspiracy of effect, but certainly not a conspiracy of intent. If you understand that the students were admitted solely on merit, then examine the backgrounds of the white students, you'll find that they were provided advantages that black children are not.'

Racism, in other words, can be experienced by people even when no one behaves toward them in a racist manner, if they are discriminated against by a system which bears the vestiges of its racist past. Jamaicans are five times as likely as Australians to be stopped by immigration officials at a British airport. UK medical schools and law firms take in disproportionately small numbers of non-white applicants. And most of this is done entirely unconsciously.

> ### 'All those who are not racially pure are mere chaff.'
>
> Adolf Hitler (who was not racially pure)

Britain has always had its share of racial tension. The Romans despised the Britons, the Britons resented the Romans, the Saxons hated the Normans and the Normans considered themselves far superior to the Saxons, all because of their physical characteristics and their social and religious customs. In the Middle Ages, Jews were discriminated against in British towns and cities, and often forced to wear a distinguishing yellow armband. William Shakespeare, writing toward the end of the sixteenth century, tackles racial prejudice in such plays as *Othello* – in which a black general is tricked into killing his young, white wife, and *The Merchant of Venice*, in which a Jewish banker is destroyed by the defences he has established in order to protect himself from Venetian anti-semitism.

The Crusades – the brainchild of the great monastic reformer, St Bernard of Clairvaux – were specifically designed to clear the Holy Land of the 'infidels'. The infamous Spanish Inquisition had a similar aim with regard to Spain, exiling or converting the Jews and Moors who had settled there over the years. All of this was done in the name of Christendom, the institutional form of European Christianity.

When Britain joined other European countries in the exploration of Africa in the sixteenth and seventeenth centuries, slave traders brought Africans not only to the West Indies, to work the colonies there, but also to mainland Britain. By 1764, there were an estimated 20,000 black people living in London, mostly (but not entirely) as slaves or hired servants.

In the nineteenth century, the heyday of the British Empire, Britain started establishing colonies in Africa itself. Africans came to Britain no longer as slaves, but as visitors or residents, although they found themselves treated by most British people with little more respect and dignity than had been the case with slaves. When Joseph Conrad wrote about Marlowe's trip up the Congo River to find Mr Kurtz in his famous novel, *Heart of Darkness* (the basis for the film *Apocalypse Now*), he pictured Congo natives as stupid or malicious, given to indulging in 'unspeakable rites'. Conrad was not being extreme for his time: the view was common, and exactly the same attitude can be seen in endless Tarzan films from the 1930s to the 1960s.

From the earliest days, the racism of British people was apparent. Colonies were run for glory and profit, and not from a sense of benevolent charity. As a result, British colonial officials told natives what to do, assuming that they knew best what was in the natives' interests (which, by a strange coincidence, was usually also what was in the interests of the colonial administration). Being both British and white, they considered themselves superior. This sense of 'superiority' was also expressed back in Britain, partly because of fear and partly through ignorance.

When the rebuilding of Europe began after the Second World War, the shortage of menial and manual workers prompted the British government to invite West Indians and others to live and work in Britain. Expecting a welcome, the new immigrants found themselves joining an already discriminated-against minority. Later, as the former colonies in Africa, India and the East became independent in the 1950s and 1960s, a new generation of immigrants came expecting to be received in a spirit of equality, but often found themselves instead simply new 'ethnic' groups to be discriminated against.

My father, for instance, was an Anglo-Indian from several generations back. More British than the British, when India achieved its independence many Anglo-Indians made use of their British passport and came to live in Britain. Although he was a well-qualified and educated man, the only work my father could find was as a labourer in a canteen, and later as a British Rail porter. (My uncle, coming over fifteen years later with almost exactly the same qualifications, was able to find work as a maths teacher, and then head of maths, in a large school.)

Racial discrimination and abuse increased to the point where, in 1965, parliament voted in a specific Race Relations Act, updated in 1968 and 1976. The 1976 Race Relations Act prohibits abuse and discrimination on the grounds of race, colour, nationality, and ethnic or national origins at work, in education, in accommodation, and in social and leisure facilities. Discrimination can either be direct ('You can't have this job') or indirect ('You can have this job, but you can't wear a turban').

The Act also outlaws discrimination *in favour of* a person on the grounds of their race or colour. It is currently only acceptable in law to discriminate for or against someone on the grounds of their race or ethnic origin where this discrimination can be shown to be part of the job itself. For example, a theatre director can insist on hiring a black man to play Othello, or a white man to play Hamlet. The manager of a Chinese restaurant can hire only Chinese waiters if this is judged essential to the restaurant's authenticity. In addition, groups working with or serving specific ethnic communities can insist that their staff come from this ethnic community. So, for instance, a black or Asian church can insist on hiring a black or Asian pastor without fear of being accused of racial discrimination.

However, statistics show that there were roughly twice as many incidents of racial abuse in Britain every week during 1994 and 1995 as there were in 1988. What isn't clear at the moment is whether this is because racial abuse is on the rise or because it's now more reported by the victims, who once considered that the police not only didn't take their complaints seriously, but actively discriminated against ethnic minority groups themselves.

According to the Commission for Racial Equality:

• A Home Office survey of February 1994 estimated a total of 130,000 racial crimes per annum, including 32,250 assaults, 52,800 threats and 26,000 acts of vandalism. Police statistics confirm that these figures are rising.
• Out of 209 accommodation agencies tested for discrimination by

the CRE in 1989, 20 per cent were shown to be consistently discriminating.

- Some 10 per cent of prisoners in Britain, and 20 per cent of women prisoners, are classified as Afro-Caribbean. The CRE considers these disproportionately high numbers to be partly the result of sentencing policy. The figures are increasing.

Reflect

In his covenant with Abraham, God established Israel as his instrument for the blessing of *all* nations. Foreigners, or 'aliens', should not be oppressed. This covenant idea, which is inherently *anti-racist*, is a constant theme in both the Old and New Testaments. It is seen, for instance, in Exodus 22:21 and 23:9; Leviticus 19:34 and 24:22; Numbers 9:14 and 15:15, 16; Deuteronomy 27:19; Psalm 146:9; Jeremiah 7:6 and 22:3; Ezekiel 22:7, 29; and Zechariah 7:10. God reminds the Israelites, in case they are tempted to think too much of themselves, that they were once aliens in Egypt. And the psalmist in exile in Babylon 500 years later reminds his hearers that they are aliens once more (Psalm 137).

'Why would we have different races if God meant us to be alike and associate with each other?'

Former Governor of Georgia, Lester Maddox

Supporters of racism, such as the British eugenicists of the first half of this century, the architects of US segregation and South African apartheid, and the numerous Christian advocates for the slave trade (of which there were many), frequently claimed biblical validity for their opinions. For instance, Genesis 9:25–27 was used to justify the ill-treatment of black people, on the grounds that they were cursed for ever to be slaves of white people because they were the sons of the disgraced Ham, who uncovered his father's nakedness (a totally false argument).

On a recent trip to South Africa, I met Dr Beyers Naudé. This courageous man was brought up an ardent supporter of apartheid, and told me that he had been impressed and convinced by the neatness and obvious sense of the racist arguments. As a preacher in the Dutch Reformed Church, he had positively enjoyed preaching on the subject of white superiority and the separation of the races. Then one day, he said, the scales fell from his eyes, and he realised that everything he had been taught to believe was wrong. As a prominent and influential church leader, this 'conversion' did not prove popular, to say the least. But Jesus breaks down racial barriers, a fact Paul makes clear when he argues that in Christ there is neither Greek nor Jew (Gal. 3:28; Col. 3:11). Beyers Naudé's realisation of this meant that he could no longer hold to the view that the races should be kept apart. Over the next twenty-five years, Naudé campaigned loudly against apartheid. His struggle won him the Nobel Peace Prize, but cost him jobs, friends and security.

> **'Nationalism as an ideology is in conflict with biblical norms because it assigns more worth and importance to one people and nation over others.'**
>
> Sojourners leader Jim Wallis

It's said that during the filming of *Jesus of Nazareth*, producer Lew Grade wouldn't have been able to tell you how many disciples there were, or how many there should have been. Nor would he have cared. Accuracy was not his strong suit. Perhaps that's why he cast a white man with blond-brown hair and blue eyes in the main part. But Grade's blunder is just one in a very long line of artistic images of Christ by white people in which he is pictured as being white. The result of this is that many people now more or less assume that Jesus really was white.

Tony Campolo recalls teaching Sunday School in Philadelphia. On the wall of the classroom was a picture of Jesus that had been there for years and years. One day it was gone, and in its place was a picture of a *black* Jesus.

'Who put this here?' Tony asked.

'I did!' One of the boys from the class identified himself as the culprit.

'But why?' Tony continued, 'Jesus wasn't black.'

'Well, he wasn't white either,' came the reply. Tony was stunned. His intellect told him that Jesus was an olive-skinned man with deep brown eyes and black hair. Yet he had always *assumed* that Jesus was white, even though he *knew* this wasn't so.

> ## 'The Ethiopians say that their gods are snub nosed and black, the Thracians that theirs have light blue eyes and red hair.'
>
> Greek philosopher Xenophanes, c. 500 BC

John 1:14 tells us that 'the Word became a human being and made his home among us'. This is concrete. It is real. But it is also very *specific*. God did not just become a man: he became a first-century, circumcised, Palestinian Jewish man, from the tribe of Judah, a speaker of Aramaic, the son of a brave young woman engaged to a poor carpenter. He came from a part of Israel which was considered less than useless, at a time when Israel itself was nothing more than a has-been, outback colony of the mighty Roman Empire.

But although Jesus was a very specific man, the salvation he offers is for *everybody*, regardless of age, race, gender, era or religion. Jesus makes it clear in the Great Commission (Matt. 28:19) that the 'New Covenant' is for *all* 'ethnic groups', *all* nations, *all* peoples, *all* cultures. At Pentecost, people of every nation in the ancient world heard about the 'wonders of God' in their own languages, their own cultural expressions (Acts 2:11). In the same vein, Paul claimed that he had 'become all things to everyone, so that by all possible means I might save some' (1 Cor. 9:22).

So the actual colour of Jesus is not important. Tony Campolo's Sunday School pupil considered Jesus black because *he* was black. Tony Campolo considered Jesus white because *he* was white. Stained-glass windows in the Philippines show Jesus with Asiatic features because most Filipinos have Asiatic features. The truth is that Jesus, a penniless Jewish carpenter, identifies with each of us in our own culture. The mistake we tend to make is to think of his identification with each of us as exclusive.

But is this really enough? Is Jesus black to black people, white to white people, Asian to Asian people, etc? American theologian James Cone thinks not. Basing his arguments on Matthew 25, in which Jesus makes it clear that how we treat the insignificants of our society is how we treat him, he argues that it's immoral to consider God colour-blind in a society which distinguishes against people simply because of their colour. In this sense, Jesus is black to *all people* when black people are abused just because of their colour. Jesus is Indian to *all people* when Indians are ill-treated simply for being Indian. Jesus is to *all people* whatever the colour or ethnic origin of their era's insignificants.

> **'When the white man came
> we had the land and they had the Bibles;
> now they have the land and we have the Bibles.'**
>
> Attributed to Chief Dan George

RACISM

- In Christ there is no black or white, 'no Jew or Greek'. In Christ, all people come together, savouring their differences as different parts of the same body.
- Racism is the idea that one group of people is inherently superior to another group of people, or that different groups of people, whilst equal in principle, should remain apart. It denies the unity of God's creation and of Christ's salvation.

Engage

During the 1980s, the World Council of Churches officially declared racism to be a heresy. There is no debate here; the Church *must* combat racism because it is a live issue and because it runs directly against the Christian gospel. So what can we do? Whether you live in an urban centre or not, the seeds of racial prejudice are all around you. All you need to do to discover this is to raise the issue in public.

**'If Christianity had asserted itself in Germany,
six million Jews would have lived.'**

Malcolm X

The first place to start is with yourself

If you think that you're not even remotely racist, you may be
deluding yourself! Everyone, whatever their colour and whatever
its origins, has some racist sentiments in them. If you approach a
group of young men on a street corner, for instance, ask yourself
whether your reaction toward them is different if they're predominantly of a colour you're not. Ask yourself how you would feel if
your son or daughter brought home someone of a different race.
Examine yourself carefully.

The next place to raise the issue is within your church

Although Christians are not immune from racially prejudiced sentiments, we are committed to a way of life in which there is no
place for a racist stance. Good teaching, which is both sensitive and
honest as well as being hard-hitting and biblical, is essential. Sermons, house groups or discussion groups, perhaps with an outside
speaker from a group like South Asian Concern or the African
Caribbean Evangelical Alliance to highlight the issues, are the simplest way of doing this.

You should raise the issue rather than waiting for it to come to
you. A white friend of mine, speaking at the funeral of a Jamaican,
took the opportunity to apologise for the behaviour of white people in general during the 1950s and 1960s, the time the dead man
and his friends had come to Britain. He could almost feel the wave
of resentment lift. It may prove embarrassing, even painful to raise
the issue, but if your church is to act against racism in the community, it is vital that it has set its own house in order.

Does your church's make-up reflect the general ethnic diversity of your area? If not, why not? Does your leadership team reflect
the diversity of your church? If not, why not? ACEA or SAC can
help you to serve those parts of the local community that you may,
until now, have been unable to reach. Or you might, for instance,

consider following the example set by churches such as Kensington Temple in London, Jesmond Parish Church in Newcastle, or Westbury Avenue Baptist Church in London's Wood Green. These, and many others, have found that by establishing a number of different congregations, individual ethnic groups have been able to worship in their own cultural style and language, whilst at the same time remaining part of one local church.

The next stage is in schools

For the majority of non-whites, their first taste of racism will have been at school, either from teachers or from other pupils. Children soak up the attitudes of others like a sponge; almost all of their early learning comes from imitation. Whilst the presence of racism in the playground doesn't automatically mean that some parents are openly racist (just as children tend, for instance, to adopt the accent of their peers rather than of their parents), it does show that society is much less free of racist sentiments than we would like to admit. It is vital that churches, which should in any case be actively involved in local schools in one way or another, find appropriate ways to raise the issue of racism in the classroom, aiming to complement whatever teaching the school may already do.

The final step is into the wider community

It is important for your church to address the issue of racism in the wider community, perhaps through seminars or publications. A survey of local racial attitudes might be a good way both of raising the issue and of discovering what people think. (Anonymity might improve your chances of getting honest responses!) This type of work is much better done by a group of churches working together, especially if this group involves any local black churches in your area. Cross-cultural projects will help to raise awareness and heal some of the wounds at the same time. As G. K. Chesterton said, the only thing to do with the ideal is to *do* it.

Further information

Agencies

African Caribbean Evangelical Alliance, Whitefield House, 186 Kennington Park Road, London SE11 4BT. Tel: 0171-582 0228.

South Asian Concern, 14 The Causeway, Sutton, Surrey SM2 5RS. Tel: 0181-661 9198.

Books

Philip Mohabir, *Building Bridges* (Hodder and Stoughton, 1992).
James Baldwin, *The Fire Next Time* (Penguin, 1963).

Chapter 8

Disability

> God has called me into an evangelistic and teaching ministry,
> using media such as poetry, writing and music as well as preach-
> ing. But often the initial reaction of people in the Church is to
> say, 'You're in a wheelchair, what can you do?'

THE WORDS OF ALYN HASKEY, an evangelist with cerebral
palsy. I've worked with Alyn on a number of occasions. On the
first, he agreed to be interviewed as part of an evangelistic event in
Derby. When the twenty-minute interview was over, the packed
thousand-seater auditorium was so moved by what he had said, and
by his poetry, that they gave him a standing ovation. But to see
Alyn in the street, you probably wouldn't think him capable of all
this. He just doesn't *look* much like an evangelist: at least, not the
way most of us think an evangelist should look. Disability is an
issue, like racism, which brings our prejudices to the fore.

Listen

What is disability? The World Health Organisation defines it as
'any restriction or lack of ability to perform an activity in the manner or within the range considered normal for a human being'.
Using this definition, the Office of Population, Censuses and Surveys estimates there to be 6.5 million disabled people in Britain:
that's more than 10 per cent of the population. One in three households is affected by some form of disability: yet disability groups
believe this survey still significantly underestimates the numbers.
Disabilities fall largely into two broad categories: physical and
mental.

Physical disabilities, and the handicaps which stem from them, can range from total paralysis below the neck to a weak heart. In contrast to the stereotype, people's physical disabilities may not be at all obvious: for instance, arthritis, diabetes, bad backs, mild polio or multiple sclerosis or cerebral palsy, deafness, partial blindness and many other things may be entirely hidden to the casual observer.

Learning disabilities – known in the caring profession rather confusingly as 'learning difficulties' – used to be referred to as 'mental handicap'. They affect mental development and function, and are experienced by as much as 2 per cent of the population, usually in a mild form. Just as there are numerous forms of learning disability, so there are many causes. Most occur before, during or soon after birth and result in lifelong impairment of intellectual function and development. They are quite distinct from *mental illness,* which can be temporary, occurs most often in adulthood, and can be treated with counselling, medication or surgery.

The causes of disability are many and varied. Arthritis, diabetes, paralysis and the loss of limbs, for example, can often be the long-term result of accidents. Physical disabilities such as deafness or blindness can occur at any stage in life, either on their own or as a result of other complications, sometimes caused by disease: bacterial meningitis can lead to deafness, and severe diabetes can lead to blindness. Learning disabilities can be caused by illness during pregnancy or early infancy, complications during pregnancy or birth, exposure to poisonous substances as an infant, physical or metabolic disorders in the body, or genetic disorders.

Disabilities can range in severity from mild to profound. With deafness, for instance, people with mild hearing loss have some difficulty following normal speech, especially when there is a lot of background noise; some wear hearing aids whilst others prefer to rely on lipreading. Profoundly deaf people, however, find hearing aids to be of little or no benefit, and if they have been deaf from birth may well have difficulty lipreading; they rely instead on sign language and the written word.

'It is not helpful to think or talk of disability as a *problem*,' warns David Potter, director of A Cause for Concern, a Christian charity that works predominantly amongst people with learning disabilities. 'For many it is a way of life and one they cope with extremely well. They might prefer not to have their disability but they want to be accepted as they are, simply because they can't do anything about their condition.' He goes on to explain that many people with disabilities find that, with a little help from the rest of society, they are able to cope with their disability as though it didn't exist.

The fairly recent changes in the titles used by certain disability organisations reflects this shift in thinking. The RNID, for instance, changed its name from the Royal National Institute for the Deaf to the Royal National Institute for Deaf People, in order to underline the fact that disabled people are *people* first. Similarly, to avoid the old stigmas, the Spastics Society have renamed themselves Scope.

'The greatest advance for disabled people has been our liberation through our civil rights campaign.'

Jane Campbell, Chairwoman of the
British Council of Organisations of Disabled People

In recent years, the tactics used by disabled people to get attention for their rights have changed drastically. Fed up with being treated as objects either of pity or care, they have placed emphasis firmly on the desire for independence. They have fought against the tendency to lump all disabled people together, insisting that their individuality and personhood be respected. A great many disabled people have begun to demand access to public utilities, employment and planning consideration as a *right*. Taking a leaf out of the feminist and anti-racist lobbies, they have resorted to direct action in order to secure legislation.

The first legislation intended to ensure fair treatment for disabled people was the 1944 Disabled Persons (Employment) Act. Among other things, this required any company with more than twenty employees to recruit at least 3 per cent of its workforce from among people registered as disabled. Someone can register as a disabled person if their handicap is sufficient to prevent them from finding or keeping work under normal circumstances. However, it's estimated that only one-third of those eligible to do so register; some, ironically, because they believe that they might suffer negative discrimination in employment if they do.

Perhaps their concern is well founded, because research shows that the 1944 quota has been almost universally ignored. Just ten companies have been prosecuted in the last fifty years, and the sum total of their fines is just £350. As a result, the government has decided to phase out the quota system in the next couple of years. In its place should come legislation making it illegal to discriminate against disabled people. Yet soberingly, government research in 1990 revealed that 6 per cent of employers admitted that they would never employ a disabled person, and a further 25 per cent admitted that they might well discriminate.

In 1994, a private member's bill aimed at guaranteeing comprehensive and enforceable rights for disabled people was sponsored by the Labour MP Roger Berry, chairman of the all-party disablement group. It was never to become law, talked out on its second reading in the House of Commons amid misplaced government fears that it would cost £17.5 billion to implement.

Disability organisations accused the government of using scaremongering tactics to scupper the bill, which received wide support from disabled people. Minister for Disabled People, Nicholas Scott, whose daughter was prominent in lobbying for the Civil Rights (Disabled Persons) Bill, resigned when it was discovered that his office had helped table the eighty amendments for discussion in the House. Many disabled protestors felt that Lady Olga Maitland MP, who helped to talk out the bill, stretched credibility when she claimed that, 'everyone in the House has one prime concern – care for the disabled'.

'It is the discrimination rather than the impairment which, so frequently, is disabling . . . so the impaired are disabled and our society is impaired.'

Conservative MP Alan Howarth in The Guardian,
26th March 1994

Disabled protestors deny that the cost of the changes required for comprehensive rights to be established by law would be prohibitive. They argue that the cost of providing such things as access to buildings should be set against the savings to the state in benefits. Those disabled people who would work if employers made provision for their disabilities argue that they would save the taxpayer in benefits what the government or their employers would spend in provision. They would then become taxpayers themselves, contributing to, as well as benefiting from, the welfare state. To this must be added the cost of carers: a report by the Princess Royal Trust for Carers, picked up by *The Independent* in October 1994, suggests that half of the 500,000 people who have had to give up work to care for a disabled person could and would work if they were offered more flexible hours, saving the state benefit payments worth roughly £560 million a year.

New government proposals in 1995 were hailed by Scott's replacement, William Hague, as an 'historic advance'. They initially rivalled a new private member's bill by Labour MP Harry Barnes, and received a decidedly lukewarm reception from disability groups. The government's Disability Discrimination Bill required only 'reasonable' access to restaurants, cinemas and shops, but made it illegal for a company with more than twenty employees to discriminate against disabled people. Separate legislation covering education and transport was initiated after protests from disability lobbyists. But serious questions were raised about the effectiveness of the proposed watchdog, the National Disability Council, given the government's refusal to grant it any powers of enforcement. As a result, it has been hailed as a toothless wonder.

'The mood in the disability lobby is one of frustration bordering on despair,' notes David Potter. 'The local authorities are now driven by budgets and targeting, with the result that services previously available are curtailed or cancelled. [Former Health Secretary] Virginia Bottomley is open to providing disabled people with vouchers so that they can buy the services which they want. However it is unlikely that the sums available will come anywhere near the costs of personal care services available to be purchased.'

Reflect

The people of the Bible didn't think about health and disability the same way we do. For them – as for most people in present-day sub-Saharan Africa, for instance – a person's health was integrally connected to the rest of their life. What was important was that they should be complete as a person. The Hebrew word 'shalom', for instance, which we know as meaning 'peace', is used in the Bible far more often to mean 'wholeness' and 'health'.

Whilst we must acknowledge that priests with physical disabilities were not permitted to serve at the altar sanctuary (Lev. 21:17–23), we should be aware that the reasons for this were entirely symbolic. The ritual ceremonies in which the priest served were concerned with representing to the people the holiness of God, and the impurity of *all* people. The priests substituted for God in the ritual, and their physical perfection was meant to demonstrate *his* perfection: they weren't intended to demonstrate some attainable standard of *human* perfection – in fact, quite the opposite. Leviticus 21:23 states explicitly that it is God who makes people holy, and not their physical or mental flawlessness.

This is shown with great clarity in Isaiah's description of the suffering servant, the person especially chosen by God because of their faith. He 'had no beauty or majesty to attract us to him, nothing in his appearance that we should desire him; he was despised and rejected, a man of sorrows, and familiar with suffering, like one from whom people hide their faces' (Isa. 53:2–3). Crushed and pierced, the very wounds of the servant were instruments of healing. The parallels here with Jesus, the fullest incarnation of the servant in Isaiah, are frequently made, but serve to emphasise that disabilities in the Bible are as frequently seen as opportunities as they are as handicaps.

This is taken one step further in the parable of the sheep and the goats (Matt. 25), in which Jesus puts himself in the position of the 'insignificants', those who appear to be the furthest imaginable from 'perfection'. Jesus, who spent his life among 'sinners', the sick and the lame, who went out of his way to touch the ritually unclean, clearly believed that people with disabilities were *people* first, relating to them in a society which stigmatised anyone with a defect. The acceptance shown by Jesus could not have contrasted more forcefully with the ostracism shown disabled people by the society of his day.

Paul follows on from the servant imagery of Isaiah, and the model of the incarnation of Jesus, by emphasising that 'God chose the foolish things of the world to shame the wise; God chose the weak things of the world to shame the strong.' He chose the orphans of the world and the ignored – the nonentities – to make as nothing the things which are valued (1 Cor. 1:27–28).

In a booklet called *No Handicaps Please, We're Christians*, Martyn Eden, David Potter and Terry Thompson reveal the same convictions: 'God will turn what we see as weakness into an opportunity to show his love and grace. When physical disability and mental handicap are seen in this light, some negative assumptions – for example that the disabled person is incomplete or "not normal" – are called into serious question.'

When the disciples of John the Baptist came to Jesus to ask him whether or not he was the Messiah, he told them to look around and to report back what they saw: 'the blind receive sight, the lame walk, those who have leprosy are cured, the deaf hear, the dead are raised and the good news is preached to the poor' (Matt. 11:5). According to Jesus, this was how the kingdom of God was to be recognised: hints of what was to come. He began his preaching career with words taken from Isaiah 61: 'The Spirit of the Lord is upon me because he has anointed me to preach good news to the poor. He has sent me to proclaim freedom for the prisoners and *recovery of sight to the blind*, to release the oppressed, to proclaim the year of the Lord's favour' (Luke 4:18–19). If we are tempted, as many Christians have been, to interpret Jesus' words as referring exclusively to 'spiritual' blindness, then we're guilty of bringing to the passage a way of thinking that would have been totally alien to Jesus. Raised in a Hebrew culture, Jesus was incapable of making a distinction between body and soul, 'physical' and 'spiritual'. He saw life as a whole.

This messianic passage draws on a rich vein of prophetic teaching that in the 'new heaven and new earth', those with disabilities would be released from their constraints and limitations (Isa. 35:3–6). In Jeremiah 31:8, Micah 4:6–7, and Zephaniah 3:19, blind and lame people get a special mention among the 'remnant' who would be saved from destruction. John reiterates this when he writes in Revelation (21:4) that in the new heaven and new earth, 'there will be no more death or mourning or crying or pain, for the old order of things has passed away'.

Jesus showed preferential treatment to those who were most ignored and despised, which included the sick, the blind, the deaf and the lame. When they encountered a blind man, Jesus' disciples asked him, 'Rabbi, who sinned, this man or his parents that he was born blind?' Jesus denied that either the man's sin or that of his parents was responsible for his condition; rather, he was blind so that through him the work of God might be revealed. The man's disability, in other words, was not the result of a wrongdoing which would make him *persona non grata* with God. Quite the opposite: it was an opportunity for God to work.

Engage

In 1995, I visited Bangkok, in Thailand. Disability is often frowned on in Thai culture, and children with disabilities ranging from cerebral palsy to something as minor as a cleft lip can find themselves abandoned by their parents. I was taken to visit the government children's home on the outskirts of the city. Built for 200 residents but now catering for over 600, those children unfortunate enough to end up there are starved of love and attention. Overcrowding means that three or sometimes four children must share a bed in appalling conditions. One assistant told me that shortages of staff and resources meant that any children who didn't suffer from learning disabilities when they came in soon acquired them as a result of the lack of attention, stimulation and love.

From there I was taken on to Rainbow House, a Christian-run foundation which 'rescues' children from the government home by negotiating to be given responsibility for them. Still shocked and haunted by what I had seen, I was brought a cup of tea by a young girl, one of about twenty-five children living there. She was aged about 7, full of energy and life, with a fantastic smile. Abandoned at birth, two years previously she had been incontinent, unable to talk and, because she had no feet, unable to walk. Now she was at school and almost incapable of *not* talking. What's more, I was reliably informed that with her new shoes on, she had become the fastest runner in her class! She was soon going to be adopted, and begin a new life as part of a new family. Yet without the help of Rainbow House, which gave her the love and resources to live a normal life, she would almost certainly have died in the government home.

This is a moving story. If we were faced with the same kind of situation that the staff of Rainbow House have to deal with, we would know what to do and have the inspiration to do it. But somehow, the fate of disabled people closer to home seems less dramatic. The problems of disabled people in the UK, and possible solutions to these problems, are less obvious to anyone who isn't disabled themselves. Yet the challenge faced by the Church in both situations is exactly the same: to help disabled people to help themselves. So what can we do?

Change attitudes

Disabled people are *people first*: they are not subjects or objects. We must strongly resist the temptation to take people on appearances, and therefore fail to appreciate either the true nature of a disabled person or their potential. We must concentrate on what they *can* do rather than on what they can't, and help them to be able to do it, both in the church and the wider community. 'There is nothing about being in a wheelchair, or blind, or deaf, or with a speech impediment,' Eden, Potter and Thompson remind us, 'that necessarily excludes people from leadership and/or service. . . . Their role in the church is, as for others, as people first. So the real question is, What is the role of people in the church and is disability allowed to get in the way of some individuals carrying out that role?'

'Steps to improve access to buildings and ensure fair employment for people with disabilities will be undermined without a fundamental shift in attitude about what it means to be a complete human being.'

Evangelical Alliance Public Affairs Director Martyn Eden

Improve access

It's tempting to excuse our usual failure to make church buildings genuinely disability-friendly by arguing that few, if any, disabled people come. But this is a Catch-22 scenario. Disabled people often don't come to church because they can't get in, and they get the impression they wouldn't be welcome even if they could. As David Potter has said, 'To know that one is accepted regardless of disability is an even greater attraction than the offer of salvation – in the first instance!' The value of friendship, especially for people with learning disabilities, shouldn't be underestimated.

On the practical side, the following need careful consideration: escorts; ramps; handrails on stairs; wide doors and corridors; lifts to higher levels; reserved car parking spaces; seats with ample leg room; spaces for wheelchairs amongst the pews/chairs; and accessible and adapted toilets. Amplification; good lighting; induction loops; signers; and reserved seats with a clear view of speakers would solve most problems encountered by deaf people in church. Clear, black and white, eye-level notices; uncluttered and straightforward passageways; bright lighting; braille or large-print literature and hymn/prayer books; and talking books would make a big difference for blind people.

Keep it simple

People with learning disabilities are usually less capable than others of following complex arguments, conceptual thinking, printed matter and variations from a routine. Responding to their spiritual needs will require the use of simple language and repetition. Short periods of concentration are essential. Avoid complex or abstract concepts, and don't be surprised if metaphors are taken literally. Encourage greater participation by the church as a whole. You might find that the rest of the congregation appreciate it as well!

Engage the wider community

It is, of course, not enough simply to clean the house. The Church's credibility as a witness will be compromised if we don't make ourselves properly accessible and welcoming to people with disabilities. But we must move beyond the walls of the church.

In the area of civil rights, we should be involved with disabled people, taking our cue from them and campaigning to ensure that those who want them are given meaningful jobs, suited to their abilities rather than to their disabilities. We should be alongside disabled people in their fight for adequate and accessible housing, education which caters for their special conditions, adequate and affordable care for their special needs, and means of transportation which don't hamper their efforts to integrate with the rest of society. We should support their demand for more braille and large-print materials; induction loops and sign language translations at theatres and cinemas; clutter-free walkways and proper access to public buildings; and a great many other things which would give disabled people the independence most of us take for granted.

In addition to this 'political' activity, there are many ways to help disabled people with their needs on a volunteer or professional level. The best way to become involved with this is for your church – as a community or as individuals – to support organisations which already co-ordinate this activity. And, of course, disabled people are no different from others in their need for a personal relationship with Jesus, presented to them in a way they can understand.

All of these things can be seen in the life of Stapleton Parish Church in Bristol. Situated near an old mental health hospital, this small Anglican church didn't have far to go for contact with disabled people, but when they started coming to church, the results were unexpected. If church members had ever been tempted to think of welcoming disabled people as an act of charity or kindness, they were in for a shock: the initial benefits were reaped by the church, not the disabled people.

Although few in number, church members with learning disabilities had a profound effect on the rest of the congregation, teaching them by example to be more friendly and welcoming with each other. Visitors to the church now receive a warm welcome, and have disabled people to thank for it. The presence of people with learning disabilities in the congregation has helped to keep services relatively simple. As a result, the atmosphere has become more informal and the 'all-together' worship encourages a greater feeling of participation and understanding than was previously the case. This has made services more accessible not just to disabled people, but also to the increasing numbers of others who have not grown up with, and therefore don't understand, traditional church culture.

The next challenge the church faced was that of access. Outside steps prevented a boy with muscular dystrophy from getting his electric wheelchair into the building. Permission was needed to convert the steps into a ramp because of its status as a Grade 1 listed building. But when permission was finally given, and the ramp built, the church discovered that it wasn't merely disabled people who were grateful for the improved access. Elderly people, and families with young children, found getting into the building easier too. When they refurbished the hall, with disabled people in mind, the church co-operated with RADAR to instal a special toilet for disabled people, with public access from the outside to anyone with a RADAR key.

Budget constraints and 'care in the community' policy led the regional health authority to close down the old mental health hospital, which it considered 'surplus to requirements', and sell off the land to property developers. Church members were shocked to discover that this would mean the demolition of a recently built community centre for people with learning disabilities. Working together with other local residents and concerned groups, they formed a trust to ensure that the centre stayed open and the needs of disabled people weren't forgotten. After a lot of hard work, and some valuable lessons learnt, the trust succeeded in not only stopping the demolition of the centre, but even extending its use to the wider community. In addition, the Secretary of State for the Environment signed a covenant insisting that the developers include six sheltered housing units for disabled people in the new, upmarket, private housing estate being built on the site of the old hospital.

Further information

Christian organisations

Church Action on Disability (CHAD), Charisma Cottage, Drewsteignton, Exeter EX6 6QR. Tel: 01647 21259.

A Cause for Concern, PO Box 351, Reading, Berkshire RG1 7AL. Tel: 01734 508781; Fax: 01734 391683.

Mainstream organisations

Royal Association for Disability and Rehabilitation (RADAR), 25 Mortimer Street, London W1N 8AB. Tel: 0171-637 5400; Minicom: 0171-637 5315.

Royal Society for Mentally Handicapped Children and Adults (MENCAP), 123 Golden Lane, London EC1Y 0RT. Tel: 0171-454 0454.

Royal National Institute for the Blind (RNIB), 224 Great Portland Street, London W1N 6AA. Tel: 0171-388 1266.

Royal National Institute for Deaf People (RNID), 105 Gower Street, London WC1E 6AH. Tel: 0171-387 8033; Fax: 0171-388 2346; Text: 0171-388 6038 (Qwerty 300 Baud) or 0171-383 3154 (Minicom).

Books

David Potter, *Mental Handicap: Is Anything Wrong?* (Kingsway, 1993).

Martyn Eden, David Potter and Terry Thompson, *No Handicaps Please, We're Christians* (Causeway, 1990). Available from A Cause for Concern.

Chapter 9

Education

FRANCIS BACON was once quoted as saying 'Knowledge itself is power.'

Throughout history, dictators and despots have attempted to control their subjects by keeping them ignorant. During Chairman Mao's 'Cultural Revolution' in China, it's said that this principle was taken to such extremes that anyone who wore glasses was considered to be an intellectual and a subversive, and was therefore imprisoned or even executed by the state. When I visited South Africa recently, black leaders told me of how the white government had consistently tried to deprive non-whites of a decent education, in the belief that people who didn't know their rights couldn't possibly assert them. All this sends a clear message: good education matters.

Listen

Many people connected with education in the UK today are agreed that morale amongst teachers and pupils alike is very low. With an increase of pupil numbers by roughly 120,000 in the autumn of 1995 alone, schools are finding that the combination of central government and local authority funding can't be stretched far enough.

Just months after teachers voted to end their boycott of the government's controversial national tests, mild-mannered school governors in safe Conservative constituencies announced that they would declare 'illegal' budgets, spending more than their central government or local authority funding allowed. Since it's illegal for schools to go into deficit, headmasters and governors alike therefore found themselves taking part in what amounts to 'civil disobedience'. Refusing to sack teachers in order to make ends meet, pushing up class sizes, they preferred instead to lock horns with the government by setting 'needs-related' budgets.

Recent research suggests that class sizes *do* matter, with appropriate teacher/pupil ratios depending on the age group of the students and the subject being taught. The evidence highlights the need for children – especially at primary level, when basic learning skills are being taught – to have close and personal access to teachers. Educational theory leans more toward group learning by instruction and experience rather than learning parrot fashion, and co-operation rather than competition. So class size is an ever-increasing key factor. Added to this, it's also clear that small class sizes reduce the pressure placed on teachers.

Teacher burn-out has always been a common feature within the education system, but it seems to have increased dramatically in recent years. As society has changed, young people have changed too, from being mere passive recipients to educational consumers who vote with their feet and their attention spans. Teachers have had to adapt in a struggle to keep up. Yet in spite of this, the majority of schoolchildren surveyed by the National Foundation for Educational Research (NFER) in 1992 admitted that, although they enjoyed school in general, they still found most of their lessons boring.

'As a teacher your role is that of an actor or entertainer,' geography teacher Julie Grant confided in *The Independent* (29th January 1993). 'It's the only way to compete with television and computer games. Children don't have any sense of wonder. They've seen it all on TV.' The same article reported an estimate by the NFER that 33 per cent of children watch TV or videos for four or more hours a day, and that 19 per cent of 13 year olds never or hardly ever read books for fun.

'Education is simply the soul of a society as it passes from one generation to another.'

G. K. Chesterton

However, change has not simply occurred in terms of teaching style. Government bodies are pushing schools to move from local education authority control to grant maintained status, by which they become independent and controlled entirely by staff and governors. In addition to this, parents have been strongly encouraged to become involved in their children's schools, perhaps as parent-governors.

Especially in middle-class areas, where residents tend to be more aware of how to make their opinions felt, this development has spurred on many parents to take an active interest in their children's school life. This has proved to be an important factor both for the encouragement and support it gives the children, and for the emphasis it places on the value of education. Parental encouragement also helps children to place what they have learnt in the context of their lives as a whole.

The introduction of GCSEs and the National Curriculum, with all its teething problems, put a tremendous strain on teachers and pupils alike. Whilst most teachers approved of the National Curriculum in theory, they were initially deeply unhappy about its precise form and the workload it introduced. In response, the government altered its content and staggered its implementation. All pupils should be following it in full by September 1997. The National Curriculum currently requires the teaching of English, maths, science, technology, PE, and a foreign language in secondary schools. These are supplemented by history, geography, art and music, which become optional after the age of 14, and 'a suitable range of optional subjects'. All pupils must be given sex education in secondary school, unless parents specifically withdraw their children from these lessons.

Schools are also required to give all pupils up to the age of 18 a basic religious education, taking up roughly 5 per cent of curriculum time. Parents can choose to opt their children out of this on grounds of conscience. Local authority schools are required to follow a syllabus agreed by each local authority's own Standing Advisory Council on Religious Education (SACRE) every five years. National model syllabuses were published in July 1994. Church schools (so-called 'voluntary schools') are not required to follow any established syllabus, and grant maintained schools can choose to follow the syllabus of *any* SACRE, even if it isn't local.

Whatever religious education syllabus they follow, schools are expected to provide pupils with a thorough knowledge of Christianity and a working knowledge of 'the other principal religions represented in this country'. RE should be presented 'from the perspective of a believer'. Syllabuses should 'not be confined to information about religions and religious traditions, practices and teaching, but extend in a religious context to wider areas of morality, including the understanding of moral issues and the consequences their behaviour has upon the family and society'. But perhaps most importantly, the teaching of *all* subjects must now by law openly include both a spiritual and moral dimension.

'The true teacher defends his pupils against his own personal influence.'

Bronson Allcot

An open letter from the Evangelical Alliance in November 1994 summed up the new regulations.

RE must move beyond a trivial presentation of the religions, which can so easily reinforce caricatures, to one which enables pupils to make a serious study of two or three religions during their school careers. Only in this way will significant learning about and learning from the religions take place. . . . It is the responsibility of schools to prepare children to live and work alongside those of other faiths and none. It is also their responsibility to help to ensure that children are equipped to make their own serious and informed decisions in matters of religion. . . . We also welcome the concern to present religion from the perspective of the believer so that students are taught those ideas and practices which are of central importance to the religion in question.

Although RE has its place, and is vital for a proper understanding of the world and our place in it, it tends to become disproportionately important for Christians. Far more was heard from the

Church about the issue of compulsory daily worship than about the pressing issues of class size, budget deficits and building repair. Trevor Cooling, Projects Officer for Stapleford House, the Association of Christian Teachers' Education Centre, sums up the situation: 'The mistake that we make time and time again is to be so concerned about issues like RE that we fail to question the messages that are coming through other areas of the curriculum and the ethos of the school.' Because of changes in education policy that dissuade schools from offering supposedly 'value-free' education – they must now state explicitly the moral basis of lessons given – local churches have the opportunity to play a full part in the life of surrounding schools and to present their opinions in a clear, open and responsible way.

All pupils are now tested in the core subjects of English, maths and science at about the ages of 7, 11 and 14. This forms part of the 'Parent's Charter', which aims to guarantee parents sufficient information about their child's school career, including an annual report on their child's progress, an annual report from the school's governors, a school prospectus, a report on their child's school by independent inspectors at least once every four years, and annual performance 'league' tables of GCSE and GCE A-level results.

League tables have come under considerable criticism for two main reasons. First, the information they contain is not 'value-added'. It is able to convey exam results, but not the extent to which a school can deliver the 'broad and balanced studies which promote spiritual, moral, cultural, mental and physical development, and prepare [children] for adult life', as required by the Parent's Charter. Their advocates argue that league tables show, and provide incentives for improvements in, the performance of individual schools. However, curriculum interpreter Jim Sweetman warns that they 'do not indicate if the quality of teaching in a school has made a difference' in the lives of the pupils being taught (*The Guardian*, 7th February 1995). Schools in deprived areas which work hard to overcome the backdrop of poverty and hopelessness may not see this effort reflected in exam results.

Second, since funding is now partly dependent upon student numbers, with funds moving from school to school with the pupil, there is a danger that parents will simply move their children from schools which perform badly in the tables to those which perform well, as much as numbers will allow. Schools are now obliged to set criteria outlining how they will decide who will be offered a place if there isn't room for everyone. However, many believe that what they see as an evolutionary, 'survival-of-the-fittest' approach to education will produce a division between the haves and the have-nots, unless good schools are somehow able to expand to incorporate the intake of the poorer schools. The freedom to exercise choice may be limited to the parents of children with ability. The less talented a child appears to be, the harder it will become to find a place for them in a good school. At the lower end of the scale, children who have been excluded from a school for any reason are already finding it increasingly difficult to obtain an education.

> **'Education is the lifeblood of the country.
> Our future prosperity as a nation depends on
> how well our schools, in partnership with parents,
> prepare young people for work and help them
> to take their place in society as
> responsible and active citizens.'**
>
> Former Secretary of State for Education John Patten

Critics also argue that the trend toward demanding good exam results – given an extra push by the compulsory testing at 7, 11 and 14 – is not all positive. Education is about a lot more than simply doing well in exams: it's about teaching people to think and preparing them for life. Setting, preparing for and marking exams takes a huge amount of time out of a teacher's schedule, leaving little room for everything else. The more emphasis is put on testing, the greater the danger that passing tests will become the goal of education rather than the proof of it.

According to the Labour Market Quarterly Report for May 1994:

- For the year of 1991–92, almost 65 per cent of 16 to 18 year olds were in some form of education, compared with 52 per cent ten years earlier. Around 1.3 million students were enrolled in higher education in 1991–92, an increase of 11 per cent on 1990–91 and of 57 per cent on 1980–81.

- In 1990–91, around 6 per cent of all school leavers left with no graded public examination results, compared with 44 per cent in 1970–71.

According to Department of Education figures:

- Fewer than 60 per cent of white 16–17 year olds are in full-time education, compared with 71 per cent of African Caribbeans, 73 per cent of Asians and 89 per cent of East Asians.

According to the Office for Standards in Education (OFSTED):

- At GCSE, 43 per cent of girls get five or more passes at or above C grade, compared with 34 per cent of boys; more girls than boys get three passes at A-level.

According to a report by the Evangelical Alliance:

- The cost of a decent private-sector education is about £6,000 per pupil per annum; the average allotted expenditure in state schools is just £2,000 per pupil per annum.

Reflect

'Give us a child until they're seven,' the Jesuits used to say, 'and we've got them for life.' This saying takes its inspiration from Proverbs 22:6: 'Instruct a child in the way they should go, and when they grow old they will not deviate from it.' The Bible is very concerned with the issue and practice of education, which it sees as instilling in people the values and moral principles they will need for the rest of their lives. 'Hold onto instruction, do not let it go,' says Proverbs 4:13. 'Guard it well, for it is your life.'

In Bible times, children learnt from their parents the skills they would need for their lives. Carpenters and farmers, for instance, would teach their trade to their sons, who would continue the family business when their father grew too old. Mothers would teach their daughters all the skills they would need for running a home and raising their own children. There were no schools for teaching these things; the knowledge was passed from one generation to the next through apprenticeship.

Specific religious education was a different matter. Most people were taught the rudiments of their religion by a specialist. Synagogues, which began life as places of worship for those who could no longer use the temple in Jerusalem, gradually and increasingly became centres of education. Children would have been taught enough to be able to read the Scriptures, and would also have had instilled into them by constant repetition the statutes of the Jewish law and the ten commandments. Deuteronomy 4:9 warns the Israelites to 'be careful, and watch yourselves closely so that you don't forget the things your eyes have seen or let them slip from your heart as long as you live. Teach them to your children and to their children after them.'

So Jesus, as he grew up, was taught the law and was expected to follow it. But we shouldn't think of this religious teaching as being like our RE today, because it covered the full spectrum of what would have been considered in Jesus' day a 'well rounded' and holistic education. The books of the law cover everything from morals to medicine.

> **'Choose my instruction instead of silver,
> knowledge rather than gold, for wisdom is
> more precious than rubies,
> and nothing you desire can compare with her.'**
>
> Proverbs 8:10–11

From the time of Samuel, and probably well before, priests and teachers of the law took pupils. Eli, for instance, taught his own children as priests, and was prepared to extend this teaching beyond his family. Samuel lived with Eli and learnt from him everything the old man was prepared to teach, just as if he had been Eli's own son. Greek philosophers like Socrates followed the same trend when they took pupils. For centuries, schools as we know them did not exist, but students gathered around a particular teacher, living with him and learning from everything he did.

In Jewish society, a noted teacher or *rabbi* (which literally means 'my master') would attract eager young 'disciples', who would live with him, travel with him, and sit at his feet while he taught (just as Mary controversially sat at Jesus' feet to learn from him: Luke 10). It was the nearest you got in village life to a place at university. Although it was 'religious education', a rabbi's teaching was expected to encompass every aspect of life, just as the law did. It was neither compartmentalised nor over-intellectual: it helped people to sort out the best way to live their lives.

Jesus never had this kind of education, and was therefore ineligible for the social and religious acceptance which went with being the disciple of a respected rabbi. When he read from the scroll of Isaiah in the Nazareth synagogue (Luke 4), and sat down to teach the people, they were amazed by his ability to speak with authority about the law in spite of having undertaken no formal study. No one was prepared for the depth of understanding he showed. They couldn't believe that they were hearing such 'gracious words' from the carpenter's son.

Jesus was keen to accept the role of rabbi. In fact, by *proactively* picking his own disciples, he positively sought it. His status as a teacher, a respected position in society, was recognised by most of the people he met. For instance, Nicodemus, himself a noted Pharisee and a member of the Jewish ruling council – Jesus called him 'Israel's teacher' – chose to address him as *rabbi*. And even those Pharisees and teachers of the law who tried to trap Jesus recognised him as a great teacher.

James understood a teacher's responsibility to set a good example when he warned, 'Not many of you should presume to be teachers, my brothers, because you know that we who teach will be judged more strictly' (James 3:1). Those who followed a rabbi followed him everywhere. They saw him at his best and his worst, and they saw how well he lived up to his teaching. If he was a hypocrite, or if his teaching did not translate well from theory to practice, then a rabbi was apt to find himself without any pupils. Education, after all, was for life.

EDUCATION

- Education should help give people control over their lives, their actions and their future. It should allow them to enjoy their God-given freedom.
- Education should also help people to gain a proper perspective on their lives, training them to live constructively and responsibly, thinking about the consequences of their actions and behaviour.

Engage

In the nineteenth century, the Church (and the evangelical wing of the Church in particular) was at the cutting edge of educational reform. Schools and universities as we know them grew from Church institutions. Even today, about one-third of all schools in this country are church schools, mostly affiliated to the Anglican or Roman Catholic denominations. Some of these are run just like local authority neighbourhood schools, catering for children of all faiths or none, in which the Church's involvement is predominantly that of helping to provide a quality education. Others aim to create a more specifically Christian education for those whose parents want them taught *as Christians* in a sympathetic environment.

On the whole, however, we seem to have lost some of our urgency when it comes to speaking up on matters of education, while parents and governors voice their anger at the government for the state of UK schools. As Christians, we have a biblical and historical commitment to provide both children and adults alike with the best education possible. So what more can a local church do?

Interest and support

'The first and most important way in which I think the local church can influence schools is by being prepared to take an interest,' comments Trevor Cooling. 'This may seem like stating the obvious, but depressingly I have to say that it rarely happens.' Your church could: schedule regular updates on what's happening in the schools in your area, supporting both teachers and pupils alike; interview the teachers and pupils in your congregation; designate one Sunday a year as special 'Education Sunday'; organise a monthly or termly prayer meeting or breakfast for Christian teachers and parents.

Once one of the most respected of professions, teaching is now vilified in some circles. When he was Secretary of State for Education, Kenneth Clarke announced that what teachers really needed was 'a bit of love'. Although not enough by itself, the value of giving teachers practical and moral support shouldn't be underestimated.

Encourage teaching vocations

In the early days of the Protestant churches, a theology developed of 'vocation' being more than simply a call to 'the ministry'. People were aware that they could be 'called' to be a banker, merchant, craftsman, etc. Today, to a large degree, we have lost this awareness, reserving the idea of vocation for those in 'professional Christian work'. We pray each week for missionaries overseas and the members of our church leadership team, and many churches have 'missionary focus boards' at the back of the church building. But rarely is anyone with a different vocation given a look-in.

The truth is, however, that God calls people to be many things, and we need to encourage each to find their vocation, whatever it might be. The chances are that at least one person in your church has a genuine calling to be a teacher. It's important for the church to recognise this calling as a real vocation, and to support it as practically as possible.

Involvement

In the present climate, which favours moving away from 'value-free' education, schools may well appreciate input from church leaders or workers who can present, as believers, a Christian perspective as part of the general RE syllabus. There is also often an opportunity to get involved in assemblies. Nothing is more effective in putting young people off Christianity than compulsory daily acts of Christian 'worship' that are conducted by teachers who have little or no interest in, or knowledge of, the Christian faith. However, an occasional assembly led by an enthusiastic minister or schools worker can be a powerful way of letting young people see something of value and relevance in the Church.

Sponsorship

The present funding crisis for education at all levels, from primary schools to universities, presents the Church with great opportunities to be of help. Pastors and youth leaders should seize this chance to develop links with local educational establishments. Book an appointment with the head teacher, offering help and support. Perhaps you could arrange to fund, or part-fund, a regional schools worker to take lessons and assemblies, or a counsellor to help students with their problems. Schools are finding support staff increasingly important, reducing the workload on teachers. You may find church schools especially receptive to the idea of a schools worker.

Even if your local school is not a church school, it will probably appreciate financial contributions, perhaps in the form of purchasing textbooks or computer equipment. (According to research published in May 1995 by the Library Association, secondary schools spend an average of £4.18 per pupil equipping their school libraries with books and other materials, whilst the average secondary school textbook costs £9.82!)

School governors

The government's strong emphasis on parental and community involvement in children's education, long sought-after by teachers, has given Christians unprecedented opportunities to guide and influence the moral, spiritual and social content and context of a school's entire syllabus. Whilst it's not in anyone's interest to turn schools into indoctrination centres, Christians should be active in making policy decisions both for individual schools and for the local education authority's various Standing Advisory Councils. CARE for Education runs a Governors' Roadshow in three different cities every year, specifically designed to help train Christian governors to be more effective. Especially if you're a parent, get involved!

Adult education and evening classes

Education is not limited to schools. Many people want to learn later in life. Some 'go back' to gain the qualifications they didn't get for various reasons when they were at school; others just want to take up something new. Many see education as a means of 'improving' themselves, or even increasing their chances of getting a job. Your church can be involved here: why not combine with other local churches to offer practical courses in such things as debt counselling, parenting, adult literacy or English as a Foreign Language. You could even run an Alpha course for those who want to know more about Christianity!

Further information

Agencies

The Association of Christian Teachers, 94A London Road, St Albans, Herts, AL1 1NX. Christian teachers will find membership most helpful.

CARE for Education, 53 Romney Street, London, SW1P 3RF. Tel: 0171-233 0455. CARE's department specifically sets out to help parents and governors.

Stapleford House Education Centre, Wesley Place, Stapleford, Nottingham, NG9 8DP. Tel: 0115-939 6270. This offers advice on resources for RE and collective worship, and a range of courses for those who want to know more about education.

Schools Ministry Network, c/o Scripture Union in Schools. A voluntary association of organisations and individuals working with schools, committed to maintaining high standards in Christian schools ministry.

Books

Trevor Cooling, *A Christian Vision for State Education* (SPCK, 1994).

Chapter 10

The environment

A FEW YEARS AGO, I was asked to speak as part of a debate on 'The Environment' at a Christian conference. I was told it was my job to provoke discussion by being as controversial as possible. Taking this to heart, I explained to my audience that in my view the whole environmental debate had been orchestrated by the New Age movement. I told them we Christians were, as the singer Larry Norman once put it, 'only visiting this planet'. Our task was to lift our sights above secular, earthbound arguments. 'Pull down the trees,' I concluded, 'and turn them into Bibles and tracts.'

By this stage I'd thought that I would have been lynched for sure. But to my horror, I found huge sections of the audience nodding their heads and actually *agreeing* with me. 'It's good to hear some sense at last,' I heard one of my misguided listeners comment.

Listen

Since the late 1980s, environmental issues have increasingly been on the world agenda. More and more research is being conducted into how our industrial and domestic behaviour affects the environment. And with the imminent arrival of the new millennium, growing numbers of people are beginning to wonder if the world we will leave to our children and grandchildren will actually be capable of sustaining them.

Politically speaking, environmental issues began to gain the prominence they deserve through the 1991 Earth Summit in Rio de Janeiro and the 1994 Cairo Summit on population control. But the refusal of world leaders like George Bush to sign an agreement on biodiversity (the continued existence of a wide variety of different species of plants and animals) points to the strong economic pressures still in place against environmental reform.

Talk of the environment conjures up a lot of different images. A baby seal is clubbed to death for its fur. A hole appears in the ozone layer high above Antarctica. Diesel-guzzling mechanical diggers chop down precious tropical rainforests. Rare species of plants and animals suddenly become extinct. Nuclear weapons are defiantly tested amid a storm of international protest. Factories pump out noxious fumes, adding to air pollution. Greenpeace dinghies criss-cross the path of nuclear waste tankers, narrowly missing being sliced in half. Oil tankers leak huge quantities of crude oil into delicate eco-systems. Land around Chernobyl is contaminated perhaps for generations to come.

These images are powerful and emotive; they are also highly complex. Like the environment itself, the issues surrounding it form a carefully and thoroughly interlinked web. Every part of the web eventually affects every other. And, as we shall see, every part of the web eventually comes back to the core issue of *poverty*.

The so-called 'greenhouse effect', otherwise known as global warming, is still under much debate. The earth's atmosphere actually has a *natural* greenhouse effect, trapping heat and light from the sun as they bounce off the earth's surface and radiating them back toward the surface again. The atmosphere is largely made up of nitrogen and oxygen gases, which don't keep the heat. So it's the other gases in the atmosphere – carbon dioxide, water vapour, ozone, methane and nitrous oxide – present in minute (or 'trace') amounts, which cause this *essential* radiation. Without it, the average temperature of the planet's surface would be roughly $-19°C$, rather than the present average of $15°C$. In effect, we would all be icicles!

If very small amounts of these 'greenhouse gases' can produce a *natural* rise of roughly $33°C$ in the average surface temperature of the earth, scientists wonder what would happen if the amount of these gases were to rise. Meteorologist Dr Robert Harwood gives the answer: 'Anything that increases the amount of these gases will tend to raise the average surface temperature of the earth.'

Scientists are not entirely agreed that the mild rise in temperatures we have experienced recently is due to humanly engineered increases in the natural greenhouse effect. In fact, there's no conclusive proof that there is *any* artificial increase in global warming. This lack of absolute certainty has led a number of governments to take only the most basic steps in reducing the emission of greenhouse gases, such as outlawing the use of CFCs in aerosol cans.

CFCs, also called 'freons', were specifically developed by industry for use in refrigerators, foam manufacturing and aerosol cans because they don't combine easily with other substances. But this means that when CFCs are released into the atmosphere, they can remain there for decades, reducing protection against UV radiation. Even if the manufacture and use of CFCs is eliminated on schedule, in 2006 (1996 for Western nations), the outer ozone layer still won't fully recover until the middle of the next century.

Joe Farman of the British Antarctic Survey, the scientific team which first discovered the hole in the outer ozone layer in 1985, warns against governments taking only limited measures in *With Scorching Heat and Drought?*: 'If we wait for convincing proof . . . it may then be too late to prevent a major and intolerable change of climate from developing.'

Increases in greenhouse gas emissions occur for a variety of reasons. Chopping down tropical rainforests (estimated to be at the rate of a football field a minute) reduces the vegetation available for absorbing CO_2. If this wood is used for fuel, it actually adds to the amount of CO_2 present in the atmosphere. If ground is successfully turned into grazing land for cattle, often destined for Western meat markets, then more methane is added to the atmosphere. And if fertilisers are used to increase the crop yield, there is likely to be a corresponding increase in levels of nitrous oxide.

'Non-renewable energy sources, which took countless millennia to evolve, are being consumed over a time scale of a few hundred years.'

Botanist Dr Malcolm Cresser

Of course, deforestation is not the only, or even the main, cause of increases in the emission of greenhouse gases like CO_2. According to a UN report produced for World Food Day in 1991, 'reproducing a growing forest the size of the Amazon basin would absorb less than 35 per cent of annual fossil fuel CO_2 emissions'.

The burning of fossil fuels plays the biggest part in increasing CO_2 levels. CO_2 emissions from the burning of natural gas are three-quarters that of oil and two-thirds that of coal, for the same amount of energy produced. It's clear, however, that future energy policies will have to depend a lot less on such non-renewable sources of energy as gas, coal and oil. This will mean a search for alternative ways of powering aircraft and cars, for instance, since petroleum-based fuels contribute significantly to the amount of CO_2 in the atmosphere. Indeed, this search is already under way. General Motors have already started marketing the world's first mass-produced electrically powered car in some states of the USA, hailing it as a 'giant leap for mankind'.

But this search will also involve a switch away from coal- and oil-fired power stations toward renewable means of producing electricity, such as geothermics, wind, water and sun. Traditional power stations operate by piping water past a heat source, turning it into steam. The steam is then used to drive huge turbines, generating electricity. Geothermal systems use natural molten rock as the heat source. At least forty countries (from a total of almost 200) are reckoned to have this capability. Wind turbines in California, though ugly, can generate electricity for roughly the same price as coal. It is thought that a new generation of more efficient wind turbines will slash this cost by almost one third. Hydro-electric power stations take water from natural mountain lakes, or pump it up from sources below, and then let gravity do the rest. The water drives turbines on its way down. Solar power is generated either by 'photovoltaic cells', which convert sunlight directly into electricity, or by using mirrors and reflectors to focus sunlight and heat the steam which drives conventional turbines.

Nuclear power stations operate in the same way as traditional power stations, but use a controlled nuclear reaction to generate heat. But whilst nuclear power is clean and efficient, it can be lethal when things go wrong, as Chernobyl demonstrated. In addition, it creates a waste product that remains dangerously radioactive for many centuries to come. And there is still no satisfactory way to dispose of radioactive waste. It can be ground and packed in glass ('vitrified'); buried deep underground; stored intact and cooled on the surface; dumped at sea (now illegal); or perhaps eventually, dumped in space. By the time it has decomposed to the level at which it's safe, the radioactivity warning symbol (☢) may be as easy for archaeologists to understand as Egyptian hieroglyphics!

With the destruction of rainforests comes the end of delicate eco-systems, built up over millions of years. Animal species, many indigenous to only one or two specific geographical areas, are disappearing at the rate of up to 100 every day. Trees also provide the main barrier against the erosion of topsoil. They soften the impact of rainfall, providing breakers against flood water and holding soil together. If trees are removed, rainwater simply runs off rather than filtering through into the soil to replenish the moisture released into the atmosphere. Nutrient-rich topsoil washes away, and green forests can literally become deserts.

In Haiti, for instance, misguided attempts to clear forests and replace them with farms left the country scarred with tracts of wasteland. Attempts to replant trees failed. The areas from which they were cut down had become desert, and the policy of US agronomists to give away free saplings didn't have the desired effect. The country's poor farmers happily took the young trees, but quickly cut them down to use for much-needed fuel in cooking and heating. Wood provides 84 per cent of all fuel in Haiti. Poverty has left agriculture severely impaired: too poor to invest in renewable and environmentally-friendly sources of energy production, Haitians are forced to use up their precious natural resources, even though this makes their poverty worse.

'It is hard for developing nations to fret about climate change and ozone depletion when their people are faced with much more immediate dangers: poverty, disease and filthy air and water.'

Charles P. Alexander in Time magazine, 7th November 1994

Poverty and environmental decay often go hand in hand. Modern industry, for example, is far more careful of energy conservation than it was fifty years ago. Yet it's invariably the old-fashioned, high-energy, high-pollution type of industry which flourishes in the Third World, exported by the West and used by poor nations as the only *affordable* means of production.

Old-style factories and industries are largely responsible for the production of what's called 'acid rain'. The term originated in nineteenth-century Manchester, where it was used to describe rain that had been polluted by the sulphur dioxide and nitrogen oxide which poured out of factory chimneys. It's thought to be responsible for damage to forests, as well as to plant and animal life in lakes and rivers.

In the centre of Bombay, the authorities have erected a huge sign which says, 'Greener, Cleaner Bombay'. Yet Bombay is filled with slums whose residents spend their lives in a constant search for enough food to feed their families. Their hand-to-mouth existence leaves no time for the luxury of environmental worries. Ecology isn't a high priority when life is a matter of pure survival. Many people in the Third World would like to be more environmentally friendly, but don't see how they can afford it. They *know* they're ruining the earth for their grandchildren; but they also know that if they can't feed their children, it won't matter how bad the earth is, because there won't *be* any grandchildren. For them, environmental worries are the hobby of the rich.

The 'population explosion' is a major concern for the environment. We already seem to be destabilising eco-systems in order to cater for the food and land needs of a rapidly burgeoning population. All the indications are that things will only get worse if the population grows. For instance, it's estimated that by the start of the next century, the population of India will be well over one billion people. What effect will its increasing industrialisation have on the global environment? It's tempting to think that poor countries remain poor simply because their populations continue to grow. This argument sounds so logical. Population control, it's claimed, would reduce poverty because there would be fewer mouths to feed. In environmental terms, this would mean less demand for energy, food and land. It would also mean less deforestation and lower CO_2 emissions.

But the problem of overpopulation can't be solved just by teaching people birth control methods and making contraceptives more widely available. In practice, poor families tend to resist attempts at population control: sex is more than just having something to do at night – when you're poor, children are all you have. So reducing poverty is not just an *aim* of population control: it's also a *method*. Improvements in material conditions, employment prospects, health care and education bring in their wake a natural levelling off of the population. Statistically, richer and better educated families have fewer children. If we are to do something about improving the environment, therefore, we will also have to do something to eliminate poverty.

According to a special report in *Time*, 7th November 1994:

- More than 20,000 species of plant or animal life become extinct every year, mostly due to human behaviour.
- By the year 2050, the number of people in the world will reach ten billion, roughly double what it is now.
- The percentage of discarded paper recycled is 35 per cent in Britain, 40 per cent in the US, and 50 per cent in Germany and Japan.

According to information produced for UN World Food Day 1991:

- Roughly fifteen million people die every year from starvation and related diseases. That's one person every two seconds.
- Over the next twenty to thirty years, food production in the Third World will have to increase by 60 per cent to meet the demand.
- More than seventeen million hectares of forest are lost every year.
- In 1980, 1,300 million people could not meet their need for fuelwood; by the year 2000, this figure is expected to rise to 3,000 million.
- The active ingredients in 25 per cent of prescription drugs come from medicinal plants, some of which are now under threat from environmental changes.

Reflect

The Church has been slow off the mark with environmental issues. Most of us are having enough trouble coping with the social agenda and the need to return to the Bible's holistic teaching. On top of this, to tackle environment issues seriously seems a bit like 'a bridge too far'.

The Church has never been very good at listening to other sectors of society. Our pride often means that, although we are good at telling people what to do and setting the agenda ourselves, we are not very good at discerning needs and responding to them. To make matters worse, the New Age movement, which Christians rightly view with suspicion, has been quick on the uptake with environmental concerns. Many Christians, wary of 'colluding with the enemy', have steered clear. The environmental crisis, however, is much too important for fears of collusion to be allowed free reign. In fact, the refusal to become involved often owes more to a reluctance to get our hands dirty than any genuine fear of 'contamination'.

Given what the Bible says about creation, the environment is definitely an issue in which we should be involved. Traditional Christian thinking has maintained three key ideas about creation:

- *It's God's world.* God made the world for himself – not for us – out of the sheer joy of creating.
- *God appointed the human race* as stewards of the world, with a special role to play.
- *The human race is part of the world.* What happens to the rest of creation affects us, and what we do affects the rest of creation.

The special role of humans is made clear when God tells Adam and Eve that they are to 'subdue' the earth, and to 'rule over the fish of the sea and the birds of the air, and over every living creature that moves on the ground' (Gen. 1:28). This mandate has caused problems. Before the Enlightenment, most Christians thought that God was present in *every* aspect of creation, and were therefore in awe of nature. But during the 1600s and 1700s, a fundamental change took place. The growth in scientific thinking led thinkers like Isaac Newton to view the world as a predictable machine. Christians saw this as an insight into the mind of God, whilst atheists and agnostics saw the need for God evaporate.

Paradoxically, though it rejected the notion that the sun, moon and stars revolved around the earth, Enlightenment thinking put human beings squarely at the centre of the universe. The Reformation idea that human beings were the *stewards* of creation – 'tenants' (Lev. 25:23) – gave way to the thought that humans, as the pinnacle of creation, could use the world more or less for their own ends. People became the consumers of creation rather than the carers for it.

Nothing could be further from the intentions of Genesis. When God put people into the Garden to 'work it and take care of it', it was a serving function that he had in mind. Human beings, made in the image of a gracious and self-sacrificial God, are given an authority over the rest of creation which is only authentic when exercised properly. People become 'great' by becoming *servants* (Matt. 20:27).

> **'Throughout the Old Testament the natural world is described as the theatre of God's glory: winds and seas, hills and plains, plants and animals are all signs of the beauty and majesty of God – not objects to be manipulated by man.'**
>
> Anglican theologian Brian Horne

At the heart of the consumer approach to creation is nothing other than plain, old-fashioned greed and self-interest: an old tale with all-too-familiar consequences. As we know, the story of Adam and Eve didn't end well: they selfishly craved what was forbidden, and when they took it, they didn't like the outcome. But it was more than just personal: the earth itself was also affected by their sin. As God explained: 'Cursed is the ground because of you; through painful toil you will eat of it all the days of your life. It will produce thorns and thistles for you, and you will eat the plants of the field. By the sweat of your brow you will eat your food until you return to the ground, since from it you were taken; for dust you are and to dust you will return' (Gen. 3:17–19).

This flatly contradicts the idea that humans are separate from the rest of creation. God made human beings 'from the dust of the earth' (Gen. 2:7). In fact, the Old Testament words for *human* and *earth* are directly linked. Although people exercise a level of authority over the rest of creation, they are quite definitely *part* of it. The sin of humanity therefore affects the rest of creation, just as the sin of individuals affects humans in general. Isaiah understood this relationship well: 'The earth is defiled by its people; they have disobeyed the laws, violated the statutes and broken the everlasting covenant. Therefore a curse consumes the earth' (Isa. 24:5–6).

'After centuries of preoccupation with the sins and sensibilities of individuals, we have woken to the corporate character of sin, especially against the environment. We are seeing the "greening" of sin.'

Theologian George Newlands

But if the whole of creation suffers as a result of our sin, it is equally true that the whole of creation shares in our salvation. God instructed Noah to build the ark not just for himself and his family, but for all the animals which otherwise wouldn't survive the flood. And after the flood, God established a 'covenant between me and you and all living creatures of every kind' (Gen. 9:15).

Isaiah pictured the final days of salvation in terms of a harmony of nature ('the wolf will live with the lamb'; Isa. 11:6–9; cf. 65:25). Drawing on Isaiah's vision of a new heaven and new earth (Isa. 65:17), both John (Rev. 21:1) and Paul saw salvation in cosmic terms. Paul spoke of creation itself being 'liberated from its bondage to decay' and of the whole of creation 'groaning as in the pains of childbirth right up to the present time' in anticipation of the future that God has in store (Rom. 8:18–22).

The idea of the earth being involved in salvation is, in fact, a central and recurring theme in the Bible. After the flood, the dominant theme in Old Testament theology is the exodus from slavery in Egypt to freedom in the Promised Land. In fact, land is central to identity in most of the Old Testament. In his book, *Living as the People of God*, Chris Wright argues that we have largely misunderstood the nature of the 'Old Covenant'. Rather than being a two-way relationship between God and Abraham's descendants, it is in fact a *triangular* relationship between God, Abraham's descendants and the land.

> **'The humans weren't the only ones who longed for liberation. The whole ecology had been moaning. The Revolution also belongs to lakes, rivers, trees, animals.'**
>
> Former Sandinista Minister of Culture, Fr Ernesto Cardenal

Given authority and responsibility to serve the rest of creation, human beings are co-creators with God of its final state. We can destroy creation by burning too many fossil fuels and damaging too many delicate eco-systems, but we can also take part in God's plan to save creation. Jesus' death and resurrection are not merely the root of *our* salvation, but of the salvation of *everything* God created. So just as we play a part in God's ongoing work to save humanity, we also play a part in God's ongoing work to save the rest of creation. It is an *evangelical* task.

THE ENVIRONMENT

- God created the world for no other reason than the joy of creating. It's his creation for us to enjoy, not our creation for us to abuse.
- We are the stewards and servants of God's creation, as well as co-workers in bringing it to its final state. Only in this sense are we to 'subdue' creation.
- God's salvation is for all creation, not merely human beings. Saving the earth is an evangelical activity.

Engage

You can't save the planet singlehandedly, but this is no excuse for inaction. When someone asked Mother Theresa how she fed thousands of children, she replied, 'One at a time.' And it's the same with the environment. In spite of the massiveness of the task, you *can* make a difference – at home, at work and in your church.

Green audit. Audit your church, office or home carefully to find out where you're environmentally friendly and where you're not. Groups like Earthcare Action and books like *50 Ways You Can Help Save the Planet* can help with this.

Recycle. Use controlled forest or recycled paper for your administration, leaflets, service sheets and weekly notices. (This paper, for instance, is manufactured from tree crops managed in Scandinavia and replaced as a natural resource. Chemicals used are disposed of without polluting the environment.) Use scrap paper in the photocopier or fax machine, rather than just throwing it away. If there are no recycling bins and bottle banks near you, approach the local council about making your church a collection point.

Use environmentally-friendly products. As well as recycled paper, you can use 100 per cent recycled, unbleached loo paper and biodegradable cleaning materials (read the labels). Use ceramic mugs and crockery that can be washed and reused, non-disposable cutlery, and fairly-traded tea and coffee.

> **'Everybody supports a clean environment in principle. Opposition only surfaces when cleaning up the environment costs money or creates inconvenience.'**
>
> Tony Campolo

Conserve energy. The more energy you waste, the more needs to be produced, often at a cost to the environment. Insulate your roof, double-glaze your windows (if you can afford it) and only heat parts of a building which need it. Use less water. Use energy-saving products such as low-energy light bulbs. When you buy new equipment, make sure that it's energy-efficient. (In the case of fridges, check that they're either CFC-free or made with genuinely recycled CFCs).

Use cars less often. Avoiding using cars, except when necessary, will lessen the amount of CO_2 released into the atmosphere from exhaust fumes. Car pools, catalytic converters and better use of public transport will also make the air more breathable. Combine with others to lobby your local authority for pedestrianised town centres, with 'park and ride' facilities.

Segregated rubbish. To help with recycling, lobby your council for segregated rubbish collection. In parts of Austria and the USA, for instance, aluminium, glass, paper, plastic, and biodegradable rubbish *must* by law be sorted and disposed of separately.

Sponsor projects. Whether it's donating a wind generator and electrical equipment to a village that would otherwise have to chop down trees for fuel, supporting the building of a hydro–electric generator by Tear Fund partners, or projects aimed at reforestation and irrigation, your church can become involved in environmental projects throughout the Third World. In fact, *any* project that makes people in poor countries less poor will be good for the environment in the long run.

Further information

Agencies

Friends of the Earth, 26 Underwood Street, London N1 7JT. Tel: 0171-490 1555.

Christian Ecology Link, 17 Burns Gardens, Lincoln, LN2 4LJ.

Earthcare Action, 22 Windermere Close, Cherry Hinton, Cambridge, CB1 4XW. Tel: 01223 412549.

A Rocha, 3 Hooper Street, Cambridge, CB1 2NZ. Tel/Fax: 01233 358830.

Books

Tony Campolo, *How To Rescue the Earth Without Worshipping Nature* (Word, 1992).

Tony Campolo and Gordon Aeschliman, *50 Ways You Can Help Save The Planet* (Kingsway, 1993).

Ron Elsdon, *Greenhouse Theology* (Monarch, 1992).

David J. Pullinger (editor), *With Scorching Heat and Drought?* A Report on the Greenhouse Effect (Science, Religion and Technology Project of the Church of Scotland, Saint Andrew Press, 1989).

Chris Seaton, *Whose Earth?* (Crossway, 1992).

Chris Wright, *Living as the People of God* (IVP, 1983).

Chapter 11

The media

THE MEDIA IS INTENSELY POWERFUL. It's generally reckoned, for instance, that Kennedy beat Nixon in the 1960 US presidential elections because Nixon's five o'clock shadow made him look shifty during televised debates. So it's hardly surprising that, twenty years later, even Americans who disagreed with his policies elected Mr Media himself, Ronald Reagan, as their fortieth President. In the *Sunday Times* supplement, 'Britain's Richest 500 of 1994', eight of the top 100 entries were in media. The supplement considered that the same is true for two of the ten wealthiest people in the world, and four of the ten richest Americans. Media is big business.

Listen

The media is growing – some would add like a cancer – in both size and power. The number of newspapers and magazines has exploded. Where many towns once had just one local paper, there are now half a dozen, mostly free. Newsagents' shelves can't hold all the magazine titles produced every week or month.

It is the same with both television and radio. BBC1, BBC2, ITV and Channel 4 have been joined by satellite and cable stations, revolutionising television. Channel 5 will soon be on air, joined as digital TV arrives by BBC3, BBC4 and another commercial franchise (all channels which will be in every home as part of the ordinary licence fee). At the same time, a relaxation of the broadcasting regulations has led to a plethora of commercial radio stations, broadcasting both regionally and nationally.

In addition, modern communications technology means that

millions of people already have the ability to 'telecommute', working from home with a fax machine, telephone and e-mail. ISDN (Integrated Services Digital Network), like a modem but very much faster and geared to transferring data from one computer to another as quickly and efficiently as possible, will eventually accelerate this process. At the moment, however, every country has its own system, most of them incompatible with anyone else's, and the cost of using ISDN in the UK is prohibitively expensive for small companies or solo operators.

The media is undergoing profound changes with the development of the Internet – the so-called 'Information Superhighway' or Infobahn. This interlinking of millions of computers allows not only e-mail communication (text-only messages sent from one computer to another via a phone line), but also the ability to 'download' information at the touch of a button through the 'World Wide Web'. Newspapers could eventually become a thing of the past, as people subscribe instead to a computer news service. Anything that can appear on a computer monitor can be distributed through the Internet. And because the system was initially designed to keep military computers talking to each other in the event of a nuclear attack, effective censorship is impossible.

Computer technology and the Internet present society with a *crisis*, a word which literally means 'a decision point'. The Internet can be liberating and creative or damaging and destructive. By enlarging its scope, *all* the present downsides of the media will be magnified, as well as *all* its advantages. For instance, as with video there's no 9 p.m. watershed, so as the opportunities for communication become greater, regulating banned material – such as hardcore pornography or racist propaganda – will become virtually impossible.

Moral guidelines have always existed to control the media. Open government censorship has gradually given way to self-regulation and bodies such as the Independent Television Commission (ITC). But though most people understand the difference between free speech and libel or incitement to violence, the line between the media reflecting society and shaping it is blurred.

'Television companies are not in the business of delivering television programmes to their audiences, they're in the business of delivering audiences to their advertisers.'

Douglas Adams

In the West we have always believed in the 'freedom of the press'. A press free from government control, it is said, is essential for the survival of democracy. Yet many people today question both the extent of this freedom and the way in which it's used. At the time of writing, for instance, the Conservatives have accused the BBC of left-wing bias, whilst Labour have accused it of being too right-wing. Tabloid newspapers seem to consider it their moral duty to try and force government ministers to resign. Self-regulation of the press has been stretched to the limit, prompting MPs from all sides to call for stricter guidelines, privacy laws or a regulatory body.

When Orson Welles made *Citizen Kane*, the studio gave him carte blanche to do what he liked. But when it was finished, they didn't initially want to release it. The film was based on the life of press baron William Randolph Hearst, and studio chiefs were afraid that he would object to the unflattering portrait . . . which he did. Such was Hearst's power that even the *threat* of retaliation was enough to make a large studio like RKO think twice. The financial ramifications could have ruined them. In the end, they released the film only after Welles threatened them with a lawsuit if they didn't.

In an attempt to curb the power of modern media moguls such as Rupert Murdoch and the late Robert Maxwell, the government has tightened control of the media by limiting the amount of total cross-media ownership (radio, TV and newspapers) that an individual or company is allowed to 15 per cent of the marketplace. But with ownership of just two daily papers, *The Sun* and *The Times*, Murdoch's News Corporation controls one-third of all daily newspaper sales in the UK. And whilst he leaves editorial decisions for *The Times* and *The Sunday Times* to the editors, he retains personal input into the content of *The Sun*. With sales of over four million, *The Sun* is the indisputable market leader. During the 1980s, it was even credited with the ability to influence the results of elections. All of which tends to make a mockery of the idea of the 'freedom of the press'.

'I get the feeling that when something appears in the paper, it ceases to be true.'

US singer and record producer T-Bone Burnett

The trend toward specialist Christian television and radio has caused worries in some quarters. So Premier, London's first Christian radio station, promised its listeners news, current affairs, music and lifestyle issues 'from a Christian perspective', but definitely 'no manic preachers, no pleas for money, no saccharin sentimentality'. And Alan Rogers, Programme Director for Christian cable TV channel Ark2, affirmed in *The Independent* (21st November 1995) their 'broad-based schedule, underpinned by Christian values, containing sport, a soap, women's interests, on-air advice and, eventually, drama and light entertainment'.

Yet send-in-the-money, touch-Jesus-through-the-TV-screen approaches are not the only concern. The most important question is, Who will tune in? Publicity for Ark2 states that their aim is to broadcast 'stimulating, humorous and warm' Christianity to people who believe in God but don't go to church. Peter Meadows, Premier's former Chief Executive, conceived his radio station in the same terms: seeker-friendly. But the predominant lesson from the American experience is that Christian stations are watched or listened to almost exclusively by Christians. This is hardly surprising since, for all their good intentions, American stations on the whole seem incapable of producing seeker-friendly programmes. When people who aren't Christians *do* tune in, they have to work hard to cut through the jargon and relate the station's message to their lives.

There is a distinct danger of both Premier and Ark2 becoming just very expensive exercises in preaching to the converted, as Christian Channel Europe seems to have been from the outset. If so, they will simply reinforce a ghetto mentality rather than communicating with people outside the Church, and so add to, rather than reduce, the Church's problems in relating to popular culture.

Six months after going on air, aware that the station hadn't managed to secure a large enough audience to cover running costs of nearly £2 million a year, Premier's trustees cut the budget in half and axed the role of Peter Meadows, their Chief Executive. In an attempt to woo listeners, the station has promised 'more distinctively Christian' programming. It will require a lot of hard work and discernment on the part of programme makers and controllers to stop this degenerating into programming merely *for Christians*.

Ark2 expects to raise its £8 million per annum budget through a combination of subscription, sponsorship and advertising. Advertising revenue is entirely dependent on audience figures: the bigger your audience, the more companies will pay to advertise on your station. Ark2 anticipates reaching 1.5 million viewers in the first year, and 2.5 million in year two. Yet existing prime-time religious programmes on terrestial TV *regularly* attract well over five million viewers. At a time when the door is already open for independent production companies to sell programmes to all channels, the question needs to be seriously debated: Is Ark2 really the best way for the Church to invest £8 million in the media? Is the Church's mandate to be 'salt' and 'light' in society best served by creating our own stations, or rather by a full commitment to and involvement in the existing media?

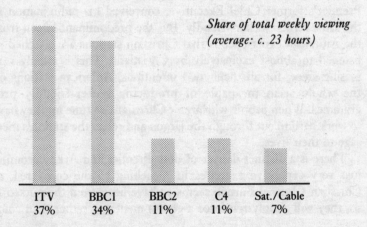

Share of total weekly viewing (average: c. 23 hours)

ITV	BBC1	BBC2	C4	Sat./Cable
37%	34%	11%	11%	7%

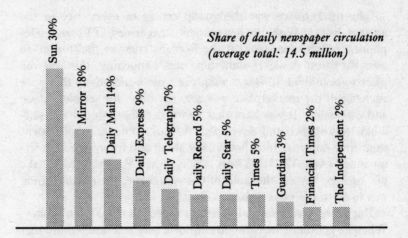

*Share of daily newspaper circulation
(average total: 14.5 million)*

Sun 30% / Mirror 18% / Daily Mail 14% / Daily Express 9% / Daily Telegraph 7% / Daily Record 5% / Daily Star 5% / Times 5% / Guardian 3% / Financial Times 2% / The Independent 2%

Reflect

Some Christians have a tendency to view the media as though everyone in them is like the stereotyped paparazzi pigs in 'Spitting Image'. We are tempted to see something rather unsavoury about the whole business: something 'worldly' and rather scary. The media seems like the devil's playground, and we need to steer clear. In order to keep ourselves holy, we should perhaps withdraw, like the Amish in the film *Witness*. Yet if we wish to be true to the Bible, this option is not open to us.

As I suggested in the Introduction, Acts 17 records that when he was in Athens, Paul 'reasoned in the synagogue with the Jews and God-fearing Gentiles' in his attempt to communicate the good news about Jesus. But that was only half his strategy: it didn't stop there. Paul adopted a 'come and go' approach to this task. So, using his knowledge of Greek culture, he also took his message to the local marketplace. Tragically, because of the experience of the nineteenth century, when it wasn't unusual to get attendance figures in the thousands at a Sunday service, the Church in the UK has become used to the idea that people *come* to our church buildings to hear about the Christian message if they really want to know. This has resulted in our neglecting the idea and art of *going* to the marketplace to put our case forward.

The marketplace was the gossip centre of every city in the ancient world. With no newspapers, magazines, TVs and telephones, people went to what the Romans knew as the 'forum' to hear the latest news. If something was happening, this was the place to hear about it. But it wasn't just news and gossip that were exchanged: the marketplace was also the place for serious debate and discussion. It was here that views, opinions, values and outlooks were shaped and developed. As Luke puts it, people 'spent their time doing nothing but talking about and listening to the latest ideas' (Acts 17:21). Which is why, when Paul wanted to take his message beyond the walls of the synagogue, the obvious thing was to go to the marketplace to do it.

But there was a second essential aspect to Paul's 'go' policy. When he got there, he chose to employ a language and culture that he knew his audience would understand and relate to. To this end, he used both Athenian poetry and an altar 'To An Unknown God' *positively* to help him 'unpack' the gospel. But this was not just window-dressing: a pagan gloss on a Christian message like sugar-coating on medicine. Paul's approach was to take the culture of his audience seriously, to engage them on their agenda, to begin where they were and with what they understood, and to move forward from there.

Compare Peter's impromptu 'press conference' in Acts 2 with Paul's speech in the marketplace in Acts 17. It is tempting for us to think that Peter's sermon represents the 'normal' or 'pure' presentation of the gospel, and that Paul's approach was deliberately to re-tailor the message to suit his audience. After all, it was Paul who claimed to have become 'all things to everyone, so that by all possible means I might save some' (1 Cor. 9:20). Yet the truth is that the words of both men were tailored to suit their audiences.

Peter addressed a crowd drawn from all over the ancient world during the Jewish harvest festival, the Festival of Weeks. They were of different colours, spoke different mother tongues, wore different clothes and considered different countries 'home'. The one thing these people had in common was their religion. So Peter peppered his speech with Old Testament quotations in order to show that Jesus was the fulfilment of God's promises and their expectations. Paul addressed a similarly cosmopolitan crowd in

Athens, one of the great cultural centres of the ancient world. He structured his speech around references to *their* culture to show that Jesus was the fulfilment of their own religion and expectations. Neither man presented the gospel in a 'pure' form: both adapted their message to the culture of their listeners.

In fact, it's impossible to present the gospel to people in a 'pure' and absolute form. We must always work hard at clothing it in the thought-patterns and concepts with which a society is familiar. This is not to compromise or water down its content, but rather to make it accessible and intelligible to our hearers, without distorting it. As the Kenyan theologian John Mbiti has said, 'We can add nothing to the Gospel, for this is an eternal gift of God; but Christianity is always a beggar seeking food and drink, cover and shelter from the cultures and times it encounters in its never-ending journeys and wanderings.'

This shouldn't come as a surprise to us. When God chose to communicate his gospel to people, he didn't send a tract. John called Jesus 'The Word'. Part of his meaning was that Jesus was God's way of communicating. Jesus came as a man of his time, in touch with his culture and a gifted communicator in it. He used stories, pictures and concepts that his listeners were at home with. Yet at the same time as accommodating himself to the culture he lived in, rather than being swamped by it or selling out to it, he presented a profound challenge to it. So profound, in fact, that they killed him for it.

This isn't the holiness of withdrawal that the Church has often practised. It's another, altogether more radical concept: an *incarnational* holiness. In the USA, the Christian subculture is massive. In terms of the media alone, Christians are often encouraged to read Christian books and Christian magazines, relax with Christian novels or Christian music, work-out to Christian aerobics, and watch Christian TV. But this withdrawal runs directly against the example of Jesus, who immersed himself in the culture of the marketplace. And one of the frequent symptoms of this 'holy' evangelical withdrawal is that, when Christians *do* get involved in the mainstream media, they are confused about what they should be doing, with the result that they often end up doing what is inappropriate.

Rather than media work (either in the 'limelight' or behind the scenes) being regarded as a legitimate vocation, it gets seen as nothing more than an opportunity for Christians to get involved in a very narrow view of 'evangelism'. But should we expect Christians in the media to preach any more than we do bank managers to put Bible verses on the end of people's bank statements, or groundsmen to carve John 3:16 into the cricket pitch? For the most part, their task is one of being 'salt' within the industry, their objective being to work at underpinning our post-Christian society with Christian principles and concepts.

All too often, Christians who have complained about being marginalised by the media have then used whatever opportunities they've managed to acquire in entirely the wrong way. And this does nothing more than to reinforce the ghetto mentality we've gradually succeeded in building for ourselves. It's important not to see the media as an avenue for any kind of formulaic evangelism. Our goal is not to try to turn 'Blue Peter' into 'The Junior Billy Graham Show'. Christians who are employed or invited on air to talk about housing or gardening, or the state of the economy, shouldn't try to talk directly about their faith. It's important to answer the questions actually being asked.

It would be wrong for Ian McCaskill, for instance, when asked about the weather at the end of the Nine O'Clock News, to answer that 'the sun will be turned to darkness and the moon to blood, before the coming of the great and dreadful day of the Lord' (Joel 2:31), or that 'there will be sun tomorrow, praise the Lord!' But if he were asked to present *Thought for the Day*, on the other hand, or interviewed for *Desert Island Discs*, then talking about his faith would be appropriate.

Engage

The media is the modern-day marketplace: it's where ideas are exchanged and opinions are forged. It's important not to fall for the old myth of seeing the media as the enemy. We should notice what's *right* as well as what's wrong with it. It can be a land of opportunity, so it's our task to be actively involved in the media, rather than withdrawing from it or ignoring it. But we should be involved in such a way that what we have to contribute to society, as Christians, is clearly understood rather than obscured. Just like Paul, it's our responsibility not only to debate in the context of the marketplace, but also to speak the language of the people who gather there.

Style

The scene is a Christian conference centre where a group of church leaders have gathered for a few days to discuss 'Reaching the Nation'. Just before the first meal, the manager asks for a show of hands as to which newspapers, if any, the guests would like in the morning. First on the list is always *The Times*, prompting slightly mocking calls of 'Ooooohh!!' from most of the delegates, who regard it as a bit too 'snooty'. Then come the other broadsheets: *The Telegraph*, *The Guardian* and *The Independent*. Most delegates plump for one of these.

Then comes *The Daily Mail*, which is considered the 'respectable' face of the tabloids. As hands go up for this, there is a discernible tutting sound, a playful expression of disapproval. But that's where the choice stops. Not once have I ever been offered the option of reading the *Mirror* or *The Sun*. Yet more people read *The Sun* than all the broadsheets put together. Along with the *Mirror*, it takes more than half the total daily market.

More than 80 per cent of all daily newspaper sales are tabloids, yet the vast majority of the Church's communication is in a strongly broadsheet style. As a result, what we have to say is often dismissed as irrelevant or obscure. Like it or not, the language of the marketplace is the language of the tabloid. To be effective, the Church needs less communication and evangelism in the style of the *Daily Telegraph*, and a lot more in the style of the *Mirror*.

Vocations

As we've seen in previous chapters, the Reformers believed in the 'priesthood of all believers', where every member of the Church understood that God had called them to a specific role. But somewhere along the line, we seem to have lost this. How many preachers eagerly claim the prayer support of their congregations to protect them because they view themselves as battling away on the spiritual *front line*? The truth is that the pulpit is not the front line. As Paul says (Ephesians 4), a church leader's task is rather 'to prepare God's people for works of service', modelling Christian values as well as the gospel to the rest of society on the *real* front line day by day. Where are the Christian television and radio presenters, producers, directors, marketers, researchers, editors, writers, camera operators, technicians, etc? Where are the newspaper journalists, photographers, editors, picture editors, etc? Why are we not encouraging people into these vocations? How can we redress the balance?

Training

Every year, when the Wimbledon tennis championships come around and all the British players get knocked out early on, the public laments the fact that we cannot seem to produce a champion. And every year, former professional players tell us the same thing: we'll never produce a world champion until we invest seriously in tennis at schools level. It takes an investment in thousands and thousands of children playing at the lowest level eventually to produce one or two champions at the highest level. There are no short-cuts. So why are there too few active Christians in key media jobs? Because the Church has spent too long avoiding the media rather than engaging it. What are we doing to inspire, train and equip Christians to serve in the 'secular media'?

Local media

Most people working in key positions in the national media cut their teeth at a local level, slowly developing their skills as volunteer assistants in hospital radio, community and local radio, local papers, etc. But quite aside from vocational training, the Church should also make use of local radio and newspapers to make a positive contribution to community life. Well-written articles or press releases about topical issues or the work the Church is doing in the community may be of considerable interest to the local media. So, as Jesus said, 'Don't hide your light under a bowl' (Matt. 5:15). Cultivate relationships with reporters and editors, getting to know them. Take the initiative.

Further information

Agencies

Trinity Square Ltd, 37 Elm Rd, New Malden, Surrey KT3 3HB. Tel: 0181-942 9761.

Oasis Trust, 87 Blackfriars Rd, London SE1 8HA. Tel: 0171-928 9422. Don't miss Oasis' media pages on the Internet – http://www.u-net.com/oasis/.

Books

Colin Morris, *God in a Box: Christian Strategy in the Television Age* (Hodder & Stoughton, 1984).

David Porter, *User's Guide to the Media* (IVP Frameworks, 1988).

Magazines and newspapers

Wired, the best-selling magazine about media technology and the Internet.

The Guardian publishes a media section in its Monday tabloid.